PRAISE FOR

Stop the Hiring Gamble

"*Stop the Hiring Gamble* is an innovative and intuitive way to look at hiring. It outlines a solid method for analyzing candidates' innate talents instead of just their résumés and rehearsed interview responses."

—J Auer, MBA, CEO of RISE Services, Inc.

"The idea of hiring based on innate abilities rather than just skills and experience is captivating. *Stop the Hiring Gamble* guides readers through this approach, offering practical methods to identify and incorporate these innate talents into the interview process. As someone who has personally implemented this approach with positive results, I can confidently say it delivers. *Stop the Hiring Gamble* is a valuable resource for anyone seeking to improve their hiring process. The focus on innate abilities offers a compelling alternative to traditional methods, and the practical tools provided can be adapted to diverse hiring needs. If you're ready to move beyond résumés and find candidates naturally suited for your roles, this book is worth your time."

—Sally Rustad, MBA, SHRM-SCP, VP of HR, Opportunity Management Group

"In *Stop the Hiring Gamble*, Dr. Nebeker draws upon his decades of experience to develop an intuitive framework to help identify and cultivate the natural strengths in others. This system works not only in business but in countless other circumstances. As a parent, the simple principles in this book have been invaluable in setting up our children to succeed."

—Rusty Crandell, attorney and cocreator of the Actively Family YouTube channel

"This book has become an indispensable cornerstone in my approach to building a successful team. I've tried my whole career to find the missing X factor in building the right team. This was the missing link for me. Through its profound insights and actionable strategies, this book has equipped me with the tools to reduce risk and confidently align new and seasoned members of my team. *Stop the Hiring Gamble* isn't just a book—it's a blueprint for creating a thriving, values-driven corporation where success is measured not only by financial gains but also by the positive impact we make on our employees and society as a whole."

—Solomon Carter Smith, president of Backroads Foundation

"Over my career, I have been in many positions in business and government where I have been responsible for hiring employees. I have had many successes but also many failures. If I had had the insight and skills taught in *Stop the Hiring Gamble*, I would have been more successful, and the organizations I was leading would have been more profitable and effective. It would have been wonderful to have Gerald there, personally guiding me through the interview process to ensure I was asking the right questions and assessing the correct definition of what I expected the employee to accomplish. Now you can have Gerald there with you by reading this book and following the hiring templates included in the appendix. It will be well worth the effort."

—W. Val Oveson, CPA, Oveson Consulting, LLC

"I'm so grateful for everything Dr. Nebeker has taught me. He genuinely cares for people and wants to see them succeed. His passion for helping organizations succeed is inspiring."

—Anne Blythe, MEd, producer and host of
The BTR.ORG podcast

"This book will transform the hiring process by integrating innate abilities with traditional metrics of education and experience. This strategy not only improves the caliber of your hires but aligns them with the organization's long-term success."

—Kathyann Powell, CEO and founder of Saving Jane, Inc.

Stop the Hiring Gamble:
Learn the Simple Method to Hire Right the First Time

by Gerald J Nebeker, PhD, DBH

© Copyright 2024 Gerald Nebeker, PhD, DBH

ISBN 979-8-88824-316-9

All rights reserved. No part of this publication may be reproduced, stored in a retrieval system, or transmitted in any form or by any means—electronic, mechanical, photocopy, recording, or any other—except for brief quotations in printed reviews, without the prior written permission of the author.

Published by

◤köehlerbooks™

3705 Shore Drive
Virginia Beach, VA 23455
800-435-4811
www.koehlerbooks.com

Stop the Hiring Gamble

Learn the Simple Method to Hire Right the First Time

Gerald J Nebeker, PhD, DBH

VIRGINIA BEACH
CAPE CHARLES

To Laurel, the love of my life and favorite implementor.

Table of Contents

Foreword 5

Introduction 6

Chapter 1: The Way Things Are 9

Chapter 2: The Problem 13

Chapter 3: Personality Traits 17

Chapter 4: The Innate Abilities 23

Chapter 5: Grower Innate Ability 30

Chapter 6: Chief Innate Ability 35

Chapter 7: Implementor Innate Ability 40

Chapter 8: Reckoner Innate Ability 46

Chapter 9: Peddler Innate Ability 51

Chapter 10: Producer Innate Ability 56

Chapter 11: Identifying the Innate Abilities 62

Chapter 12: Individual Differences 67

Chapter 13: Innate Ability Hiring 72

Chapter 14: Right People, Right Time 83

Chapter 15: Four Quadrants 91

Chapter 16: When it Works 96

Chapter 17: Conclusion 100

Chapter Notes 102

Appendix A: The Hiring Template 115

Appendix B: The Promoting Template 134

Foreword

The concepts in this book are based on my observations of employees over the last forty years as a boss and the research I've done to help understand human behavior. I have puzzled over why some people succeed and others fail in their jobs. I've read countless management books, attended seminars and trainings, and taught doctoral students about team dynamics. It wasn't until I started noticing that some people were hardwired to be successful in their role and others were not that the answers came. I initially thought training could increase the aptness of employees to their roles. I've concluded it has minimal impact in the end. People can learn the tasks required of a job but not the instincts often needed to excel. I've tried to remediate people over the years and usually felt I was working harder for their success than they were. The older I get, the more I find myself on the "nature" side of the nature versus nurture quandary. In America, we are often taught we can be anything we want—true if we have the brains and innate ability to match and false if not. Rather than cry about what we aren't or what our employees lack, I hope this book will provide a reason to celebrate our God-given abilities. The challenge is to identify our and our employee's innate abilities, which is the goal of this book. The scenarios enclosed are based on actual people and events. Names and circumstances have been changed to protect confidentiality.

Introduction

> "Our fatigue is often caused not by work,
> but by worry, frustration, and resentment."
> —Dale Carnegie

Getting people into the right seats in your company is challenging. Everyone experiences hiring debacles if they have been in business long. I have had plenty; despite great experience, education, and an impressive interview, some hires turned out to be disastrous. I have also promoted people because they were stellar in one role, but they failed in their new position. I joked with my VP of human services that the odds of getting the right person in the correct position were like shooting craps. Research backs my claim.[1]

I have spent almost forty years building a company that supports people with developmental disabilities. We are currently located in six states and employ thousands of people. I have been blessed to be its founder and president. I also founded an employer fiscal agent company that was the first of its kind to go national. At present, the company employs several hundred employees, has contracts with twenty-eight states, and processes close to $1 billion annually of Medicaid support dollars. I sold the company after twenty-five years, reaping the financial benefits of an equity stake in a profitable company.

My experience has given me the advantage of growing two organizations from scratch and interacting with personnel at every level. In addition, over the last twenty years, I have provided management coaching for many experienced and young business leaders trying to make a mark on the world.

I have seen and experienced a range of personal hiring wins and failures. How many have hired a self-proclaimed vampire or a director who solicits alcohol from coworkers within the first few hours on the job? Or, my favorite, a supervisor with the power to sexually harass through telepathy. But this book isn't about humor in hiring. It's about increasing the odds of hiring or promoting the right person.

Many years ago, I employed Susan. She was, in every respect, an exemplary employee. She checked all the boxes in caring for the vulnerable individuals my company supports. She was so good that she was the logical person to advance into a leadership position. Sadly, Susan bombed. A month before her resignation, she asked to meet with me. She looked frustrated and frazzled and said, "Gerald, just tell me what you want me to do." At the time, I didn't realize her plea wasn't so much a request for a list of tasks; instead, it was a cry for help. She was self-identifying her innate ability, and I didn't recognize it. Had I had the knowledge I have now back then, I could have prevented a failure for her and the company.

Much like a sergeant waiting for orders, Susan needed instruction from a superior officer. She needed someone to tell her what to do. I failed Susan by assuming she could figure it out, create objectives, and organize others to accomplish them. When she quit, the company lost a valuable employee. Sadly, I repeated this pattern many times in the subsequent decades, advancing excellent employees or hiring based on interviews and résumés alone, only to see them flop. Don't get me wrong; I have hired fantastic people, but frankly, knowing what I know now, that was dumb luck.

I finally figured out what was going on. I realized that

peoples' success in their corporate roles had little to do with their homelife, education, experience, attitude, or personality. It is much more fundamental than that. It is something they are born with. It is their innate ability.

CHAPTER 1

The Way Things Are

> "Because things are the way they are,
> things will not stay the way they are."
> —Bertolt Brecht

The CEO of a company I work with told me about an executive they hired recently. He interviewed well and had a fantastic résumé and relevant experience. His letters of recommendation were solid, and his references checked out. He was a disaster. It's taken the company months to undo the damage he did to the company's reputation in the few weeks he was on the job.

The company (and pretty much every other company) follows the same game plan in hiring executives. Applications come in the door (how varies), résumés are reviewed, interviews are conducted, letters of recommendation are read, and references are called. Hiring procedures are akin to religious observance, and messing with them is sacrilege. The belief is if you adhere to the hiring rites, the employer gods may smile upon you and grant you a great addition to your team. It doesn't always work out that way, but with a lack of an alternative process, companies keep doing the same thing over and over and hoping irrationally for different results.

I am sure you know some of the résumés you review are padded, right? According to Findlaw.com, 36 percent of people pad their résumé.[1] And, did they really graduate from the universities they list, or are they one of the 100,000 each year that George Gollin of the Council for Higher Education Accreditation claims bought a fake degree.[2] Will some of them apply with your company? Likely. So, should you make hiring decisions based solely on the strength of a résumé?

I remember when my COO hired a woman with a wonderful résumé. She had a doctorate in educational psychology from a well-known university and supplied a copy of her diploma as proof. When I met her, something seemed off. She didn't have the knowledge base her title would indicate. I questioned her about her program, which she answered superficially, so I dug deeper. It turns out that the university did not have a record of her. She must have bought her degree online; therefore, her Ivy League diploma was fake. When confronted with this information, she defended herself by saying, "Oh, I must have given you my draft résumé." We fired her.

Go online and search "buy a college diploma" or something similar. You will be surprised how many sites, for a fee, will supply you with a diploma (the university of your choice in some cases), transcripts, and even letters of reference from some of "your professors." You are in good company if you've ever been duped by an employee with fake credentials. It turns out that MIT discovered its dean of admissions, who worked in that role for almost a decade (twenty-eight years as a university administrator), didn't graduate from the three colleges she listed on her résumé. In fact, she only completed a couple of college classes. As *The Harvard Crimson* reported, she resigned when the deception came to light, likely to avoid termination.[3] Ironically, MIT lost a competent, almost three-decade employee, and she was disgraced.

Do you realize applicants can read most or all the interview questions companies typically ask and how they should answer them? I didn't until I started writing this book. It never occurred to me. Go online and type, "Job interview questions and how to answer them" in your search engine.[4] You can't know who prepped in this manner, and maybe it doesn't matter if you consider the fact when someone impresses you with their answers. Does that mean the applicants who give the best answers are the ones with the best memorization skills? How someone answers shouldn't be the single determinant of whom you hire.

Are you aware that whoever interviews first or last will have a greater chance of being hired?[5] The reason is that two interesting phenomena come into play: primacy and recency bias. Primacy bias is the tendency to remember what we learned first, and recency bias is the inclination to remember things better that happened most recently. If you interview twenty candidates, the first and last interview will be more likely remembered, and the other eighteen will be a blur. What if the best candidate is the one who interviews in the middle? Should you still conduct serial interviews?

Do letters of recommendation and references influence your hiring? Helen De Cruz, a Danforth Chair in the Humanities at St Louis University, believes they are a waste of time and of no evidential value.[6] I agree. Let's be honest. When was the last time you got a nasty letter of recommendation or had a negative reference check? Have you ever? I never have and I've read hundreds. If you read a stack of them, don't they all read about the same? Granted, some of the authors are better writers than others, but is that relevant to your candidate? You are hiring the applicant, not the author of the reference. So . . . letters of recommendation are valuable because . . . ?

The consequences of hiring the right person or the wrong person are monumental. Companies need to do everything they can to increase the chances of getting it right. If you continue to hire the way you always have, you will continue to get the results you have always gotten. What a bad hire can destroy in a few weeks will take the company a year to fix. You can increase the odds of hiring right by employing the techniques in this book.

CHAPTER 2

The Problem

> "Focus on the solution,
> not on the problem."
> —Jim Rohn

In 1969, Canadians Dr. Laurence Peter, an educator, and Raymond Hull, a playwright, wrote a satirical book called *The Peter Principle*.[1] The book struck a chord; it was a bestseller for thirty-three weeks in the US. It has been translated into more than twenty languages, has sold millions of copies worldwide, has been the basis of research and commentary, and is as relevant today as when it was published. Whether you've read the book or not, you have probably heard the term "the Peter principle." It is ubiquitous in business—employees are promoted until they reach their level of incompetence. They then stay at that level.

Why do employers and employees experience the Peter principle? Aren't the employees capable? Aren't they bright enough? Can't they learn new skills? The answer to these questions is "yes." Then why do they fail? It's because their bosses made the same mistake I did with Susan, whom I described in the introduction; they were promoted without regard to their innate ability. It's not a matter of competence, attitude, or training; it's a matter of hard-wiring. For example, I can take singing lessons and practice regularly (I did for a year) and become knowledgeable to a degree (which I did), but I'll never be better than mediocre. I can practice hours every day for years, but I'll never experience a curtain call at The Met. I'm not being modest; I don't have the pipes for it. The way to avoid the Peter principle is for employers to implement hiring and promoting based on innate abilities.

There are likely many innate abilities, but my research and experience point to six crucial ones in business: grower, chief, implementor, reckoner, peddler, and producer. I will discuss each in detail in subsequent chapters. I chose these labels carefully to avoid confusing the ability with a job title like accountant or using terms like leader or manager.

Regardless of education or experience, if a person works in a role with expectations different from their innate ability, they will be less effective, dread work, and likely fail. Or perhaps worse, they will become a casualty of the Peter principle and be stuck in that position. When bosses understand innate abilities, they hire smarter and better and align job expectations with natural talents.

Education and experience are important, but they don't predict job success. Have you ever hired someone (or been that someone yourself) who didn't work out despite having glowing references, an appropriate degree, and related experience? To make matters worse, when the employee moved on from you, were they wildly successful with another company, doing the same job they failed at with you? Was it them, you, or something different? I wager it was something different; my bet is the difference was that their innate ability didn't match your expectations for the role.

I've seen this dozens of times. For example, several years ago, CEO Julie hired a VP of human resources, Ted. Ted had a degree in HR, was SHRM certified, had a lot of previous experience, and came highly recommended. Everyone loved Ted, and he did a great job making sure their existing HR policies were in top shape. But Julie's company needed more, someone who would proactively lead the HR team. After counseling and warnings, nothing changed. Julie fired Ted, not because he wasn't competent or popular but because he didn't meet the company's needs. Thirty days later, Ted landed a new job at a different company as their new VP of HR. He has worked in that position for many years, and the company and Ted are very happy with each other.

It was the same Ted in the same role. On paper, the job, requirements, and duties were similar. Ted failed with Julie's company because they needed someone with a different innate ability. He was successful with the new company because his innate ability was precisely what they needed. Why the difference? Julie hired Ted with the typical procedure—got an application and résumé, verified his education and experience, checked references, and conducted an interview. She was impressed; he checked all the boxes. The problem was Julie didn't have all the right boxes.

When you need to hire someone, you can look externally or internally. If externally, you place an ad, accept applications, review résumés, and conduct interviews. If internally, you might conduct interviews or engage in a more formal procedure, typical in larger companies. But often, bosses advance someone because they know them, circumventing vetting procedures.

Following the standard procedure, whether external or internal, it's a gamble. In an article published by LinkedIn, Lou Alder states that your odds of hiring a top performer are little better than 50 percent with an internal candidate and as low as 17 percent with a stranger.[2] When faced with these terrible odds, companies double down on hiring protocols, increase pressure on the HR team, enact more rigorous vetting, or engage a headhunter. These efforts do little to increase the odds of getting the right person because they do not account for innate ability.

The solution is to ascertain what innate ability you need

in addition to their résumé's content. This book will teach you about the six innate abilities, how to identify them in candidates and current employees, and how to better establish your expectations for various job positions so you can flip the odds in your favor. Before learning about innate abilities, we need to review personality traits. Many people wrongfully assume that personality assessments like the Myers-Briggs or Big Five, for example, are good screeners of candidates to determine job fit. They are not.

CHAPTER 3

Personality Traits

"Personality is an unbroken series of
successful gestures."
—F. Scott Fitzgerald

The fact that people are different from one another is no surprise. Psychiatrist Carl Jung in the 1920s and psychologists Gordon Allport and Henry Odbert in the 1930s attempted to explain those differences by identifying personality types. Others followed their lead and created the field of personality psychology, which studies how personality develops. One of the debates is whether people were born with or learned (nature versus nurture) their personality.

Many companies wrongfully use personality assessments as if they were DNA tests to screen applicants to determine the goodness of fit for the job they are hiring for. However, personality traits are not abilities. They are more about who people are, and scores may evolve with age and life events. An innate ability is what people do. It's how you naturally act; you are born with it, and circumstances won't affect it. On the surface, they may seem similar, but they are very different.

This chapter is devoted to two common job screening assessments of personality: the Big Five and Myers-Briggs. It is important to know what they are, the results they give, and their value, or not, in the job interview process. Spoiler alert: their value lies in helping explain individual differences, not job placements. They weren't designed for that.

The Big Five grew out of the work of D. W. Fiske in 1949 and was later expanded by others. A Big Five assessment asks 240 questions. How a taker answers them determines how high or low they are on five personality dimensions: openness, conscientiousness, extraversion, agreeableness, and neuroticism.[1] The most highly regarded standard test for measuring the Big Five is Costa and McCrae's NEO-PI-R.[2] A brief description of the results is in table 1.

Table 1

	Openness	Conscientiousness	Extraversion	Agreeableness	Neuroticism
High	Creative Imaginative Spontaneous	Thoughtfulness Planful Organized	Sociability Fun-loving Energetic	Kind Trusting Helpful	Pessimistic Instability Anxious
Low	Practical Prefers routine	Impulsive Disorganized Procrastinate	Reserved Thoughtful Introverted	Self-centered Suspicious Uncooperative	Calm Confident Optimistic

The Big Five has been widely studied, and a body of research supports its validity and reliability. Still, even its advocates recommend it only be used to get to know an applicant better, not to make final hiring decisions.[3]

The Myers-Briggs assessment is a pop-psych phenomenon. It is the most widely used personality assessment globally, with approximately two million people taking it annually. It was initially developed by Katharine Cook Briggs and her daughter,

Isabel Briggs Myers, in the 1920s. Their goal was to change the world through learning and appreciating others' personality differences.[4]

The Myers-Briggs asks ninety-three questions and measures four personality dimensions: introversion/extraversion, sensation/intuition, thinking/feeling, and judging/perceiving. These factors create sixteen combinations that purportedly identify a taker's personality, shown in table 2.[5]

Table 2

ISTJ	**ISFJ**	**INFJ**	**INTJ**
Factual	Detailed	Committed	Independent
Practical	Traditional	Creative	Visionary
Organized	Service-minded	Determined	Original
Steadfast	Devoted	Idealistic	Global
ISTP	**ISFP**	**INFP**	**INTP**
Logical	Caring	Compassionate	Independent
Realistic	Adaptable	Original	Theoretical
Adventurous	Gentle	Creative	Analytical
Self-determined	Harmonious	Empathetic	Reserved
ESTP	**ESFP**	**ENFP**	**ENTP**
Activity-oriented	Enthusiastic	Creative	Enterprising
Versatile	Friendly	Versatile	Outspoken
Pragmatic	Cooperative	Perceptive	Challenging
Outgoing	Tolerant	Imaginative	Resourceful
ESTJ	**ESFJ**	**ENFJ**	**ENTJ**
Logical	Thorough	Loyal	Logical
Systematic	Responsible	Verbal	Strategic
Organized	Detailed	Energetic	Fair
Conscientious	Traditional	Congenial	Straightforward

Interestingly, despite being one of the world's most widely used personality assessments, there is very little science behind it.[6] It is based on observations, not scientific research. Yet some companies wrongfully believe it is the gateway to understanding personnel. They require all applicants to take it, hire based on it, use it to create work groups, and sadly, don't promote some people because of their four-letter code results.[7] The Myers-Briggs is not a blood test to determine differences; peoples' life circumstances at the time they take it can affect their score.

If you are like me, when you read the Big Five and Myers-Briggs results descriptions, you might think they read like zodiac sign descriptions. You wouldn't be wrong. I include the astrological signs for fun in table 3.[8] Could using astrological signs in job screening be as valid as a personality test? I'm not going there, but believe it or not, some companies have used astrology in their screening process.

Table 3

Aquarius	**Pisces**	**Aries**	**Taurus**
Progressive	Compassionate	Courageous	Reliable
Original	Artistic	Determined	Patient
Independent	Intuitive	Confident	Practical
Humanitarian	Gentle	Enthusiastic	Devoted
Gemini	**Cancer**	**Leo**	**Virgo**
Gentle	Tenacious	Creative	Loyal
Affectionate	Imaginative	Passionate	Analytical
Curious	Loyal	Generous	Kind
Adaptable	Emotional	Warmhearted	Hardworking
Libra	**Scorpio**	**Sagittarius**	**Capricorn**
Cooperative	Resourceful	Generous	Responsible
Diplomatic	Powerful	Idealistic	Disciplined
Gracious	Brave	Humorous	Self-control
Fair-minded	Passionate	Impatient	Manager

Should you throw out personality assessments in hiring? Not necessarily. They might help you get to know the candidates better. But you might as well ask an applicant's astrological sign, learn their "personality color" from the Color Code—another personality test—or heaven forbid conduct a phrenology exam.[9] The results are better shared at an office get-to-know-you-better party than making hiring decisions. As Emma Goldberg pithily states,[10]

> Personality assessments short-circuit the messiness of building what is now referred to as a "culture." They deliver on all the complexities of interpersonal office dynamics, but without the intimate, and expensive, process of actually speaking with employees to determine their quirks and preferences.
>
> They appeal also, perhaps, for the same reason astrology, numerology and other hocus-pocus systems do: because it's fun to divide people into categories. They tap into the angst of the "where y'all sitting" meme, the hunger to know where you belong in the lunchtime cafeteria scene.
>
> Myers-Briggs makes human resources into an algorithm: Give your employee an online quiz, and within minutes you'll know whether they're social (E) or quiet (I), interested in details (S) or the big picture (N). Forget all the messy, expensive team off-sites and one-on-ones — how much easier is it to compress assessments into four little letters, puzzle pieces on the page? It's H.R. tailor-made for the BuzzFeed quiz generation.

In his marvelous book, *The Lost Art of Healing*, Dr. Bernard Lown makes a profound point that medicine currently relies heavily on clinical tests and is light on talking with patients. He advocates conversation in addition to tests for more accurate diagnoses of what is really going on.[11] I recommend the same in hiring and promoting. You can certainly give applicants a personality test. They are easy to administer and score, and you will get a list of attributes associated with the score, but they won't get you to the true predictor of job suitability. That comes from matching a candidate's innate ability with the job. As you will learn later in this book, you won't discover a person's innate ability through a slick online thirty-six-question assessment. You'll learn it through talking with them. Yes, very low-tech. Applicants, and everyone else for that matter, will tell you what their ability is. We wear our innate abilities on our sleeves. They are easily discoverable if you know what you are listening for. Innate abilities will better predict job success than the results of any personality assessment.

CHAPTER 4

The Innate Abilities

> "The most important kind of freedom is to be what you really are."
> —Jim Morrison

Various business books touch on some of the innate abilities with different labels. Some use the terms "leadership" and "management" interchangeably as nouns or verbs, for example. But they aren't the same thing. Others tout that you can gain an ability if you don't already have it. Not likely. We can work on skills we don't naturally have all our lives and end up with well-practiced weaknesses. We might become good enough to get by, but work will be more tedious than if we were working in the zone of our innate ability. People working in roles outside their innate ability are like cars with one dead sparkplug. Sure, you can get by. But people, like cars, work best when all cylinders are firing synergistically together according to their innate ability.

Through research and experience, I've identified the following six primary workplace innate abilities: grower, chief, implementor, reckoner, peddler, and producer. These abilities are seen in adults regardless of their sex, age, or racial, ethnic, or socioeconomic backgrounds. As you read the descriptions, who on your team comes to mind? Which of these is you?

Grower: the entrepreneurs and risk-takers. They are typically creative, freewheeling, idea-focused, and forward-thinking. They don't like accountability. Their desks and offices are often messy and in disarray. New opportunity creation is their primary work product.

Chief: the leaders. Many political, religious, and company heads have this ability, but they can exist at all company levels. They are people-focused. They take charge, and people naturally follow them. They develop instructions for others to follow. Directing and organizing others is their primary work product.

Implementor: the managers of assignments. They are task-focused and can be found at all company levels. Given instructions to carry out, they will do so with gusto. Execution is their primary work product.

Reckoner: the risk-averse. They like rules and everything in its place. People with this ability often end up as accountants, editors, and attorneys. They are rules-focused. Their offices and desks are typically neat and well-organized. Accountability is their primary work product.

Peddler: the salespeople. They are focused on promoting. Relationship-building is their primary work product.

Producer: the workers. They want to do their job and go home. They have little emotional investment in the job. They are outside-of-work-focused. Performing tasks that the company gets paid for is their work product.

People with each of the innate abilities are essential to an effective team. One way to remember them and the role they play is by imagining a team organizing to climb a mountain:

- ◇ The grower is the person who mortgages their home to buy the mountain (or at least all of the equipment), and it is their idea to climb it.

- ◊ The chief is the person who organizes a team to climb the mountain.
- ◊ The implementor is the person who ensures everyone packs a lunch on the hike.
- ◊ The reckoner is the person who brings a map to ensure the group follows the right trail.
- ◊ The peddler is the person who sells the movie rights to the experience.
- ◊ The producers are the people who carry everyone else's water.

Another analogy might add clarity. In a professional football team,

- ◊ The grower is the team owner.
- ◊ The chief is the coach.
- ◊ The quarterback is the implementor.
- ◊ The reckoners are the people keeping statistics.
- ◊ The peddler is the one selling advertising and sponsorships.
- ◊ The producers are the players.

A third way to understand the abilities is to consider synonyms and stereotypical C-Suite job titles associated with them, but the innate abilities aren't necessarily correlated with C-Suite positions:

Grower—Entrepreneur—Dreamer—Creator—Owner
Chief—Leader—Delegator—Organizer—CEO
Implementor—Manager—Overseer—Assembler—COO
Reckoner—Accountant—Analyst—Auditor—CFO
Peddler—Salesperson—Agent—Hawker—CSO
Producer—Worker—Doer—Staff—(not typically in the C-Suite)

Do you recognize yourself? How about some of your team members?

It's easy to think that the abilities are ranked in value. Granted, earnings are associated with the position, but each innate ability is equally important and interdependent. A successful organization will have people with all six abilities, complementing and sometimes creating a healthy friction.

Too many with the same innate abilities will cause problems. For example, an organization with all growers or all reckoners will die a rapid death. The former is focused on expansion, and the latter is focused on the rules; neither is focused on the business of the company. An organization with all chiefs or implementors will die a slower death. They will manage it to death. An organization with all peddlers will drive everyone crazy and fold because selling doesn't actually involve doing what the company gets paid for. An organization with all producers would have never been organized in the first place.

People can perform the tasks of the other abilities for a time, but it doesn't feel natural. I was the only employee when I started my first company, so I was the "chief cook and bottle washer," true to the idiom. I was its only employee until I hired Reva, a reckoner, and boy, was I relieved. I am a grower, and while I could do the accounting, it wore me out; I hated it and was not good at it.

Your innate ability is your zone. When you are in your zone, it is invigorating. Veer out of that lane, and work becomes a drudgery. That is one of the diagnostic tests to identify your innate ability. What do you default to? Which do you enjoy the most or find least taxing? Demarcation isn't always clear or practical; however, your innate ability is that worn groove where you feel most comfortable. It is your default. You don't have to think about it because it comes naturally.

Still don't know what you are? In an email or letter, ask

a bunch of people who know you well, people you work with, friends, and relatives. Write something like, "I'm not fishing for anything; I just want to know what you see in me that I am naturally good at." If they call you, all concerned and wondering if you are depressed or going through a midlife crisis, reassure them that you are just working through an assignment in a book and would value their honest opinion.[1] Generally speaking, as you read the feedback, you will see a pattern in their comments that should give you a big hint. You will have to interpret their feedback and see which of the innate abilities the comments describe. You will read some compliments, like how talented, nice, or humble you are or what a great parent you are, but look beyond those comments. If you are a grower, you may read that you are very creative or a risk-taker. If you are a chief, people may comment on what a good leader you are or how people naturally follow you. If you are an implementor, you may read how you can easily see how to get things done. If you are a reckoner, people may write how good you are with numbers or requirements. If you are a peddler, you may read how good you are with people or how persuasive you can be. If you are a producer, you may read how good you are at volunteering for things at church or community or how dedicated you are to your family.

There aren't hard lines between the abilities, and many people identify with two, although most feel they are stronger in one than the other. I often ask people to rank the abilities from most to least like them, which most can do easily. Consider each ability as a spectrum that can overlap with others, as illustrated in figure 1. For example, some chiefs can be creative and entrepreneurial, hallmarks of a grower, and task-oriented, the trait of implementors. The difference is the frequency and consistency. Many growers can be excellent leaders, the attribute of chiefs, and be good at inspiring people, the ability of peddlers. Again, the regularity will be less than for a pure chief or peddler.

People can also emulate the other abilities if they must, typically because that ability is not innate in any of their team members. Some of us have practiced weaknesses well by emulating the other abilities. Many do it for years, which contributes to work burnout.

Figure 1

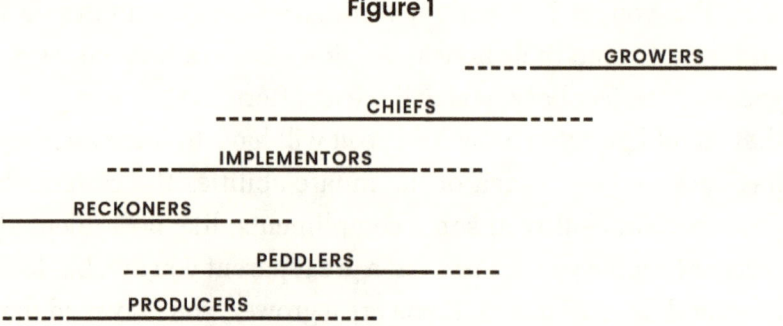

Knowing what your innate ability is and the innate abilities of your current team members is important. If you have any missing innate abilities, you need to add those to your team if you can. Each of the six innate abilities will be explored in detail in the subsequent chapters.

I do need to talk about creativity. Although it might seem like it, creativity is not a distinct innate ability but more a subset. I have interacted with hundreds of people with different innate abilities and found creative and noncreative people in each category. I appreciate the creativity of my reckoner travel agent, who figures out the best vacation plans for me, and I am comforted that my reckoner airline pilot who flies me there is not creative. I want my pilot to follow safety protocols with precision on every flight.

Creative people are full of ideas, and I love hanging out with them. I find them very stimulating because I'm a creative person too. My favorite thing to do is to brainstorm solutions. As a grower, I don't want to be responsible for implementing any of them, but I love to spin ideas. I periodically gather a group of known creative people in my company with different innate abilities. I call it a spinners meeting. The purpose isn't to solve any problems now or implement anything but to simply kick ideas around. People with various innate abilities sharing their perspectives ultimately creates better approaches and solutions, and many companies do these types of meetings.

Spinner meetings can drive noncreative people nuts. For example, in strategic planning sessions, I have participants engage in idea generation prior to deciding upon the goals. It's a free-flow thought process. The creative types in the room are participative, whipping out all kinds of ideas. The noncreative folks say little, if anything at all. After one such meeting, Jessi, a noncreative implementor who didn't speak at all during the entire meeting, said afterward, "All this brainstorming is fine, but what do you want me to do?" Since most people can self-identify the degree of their creativity, had I asked Jessi, she would have said she wasn't creative. I wouldn't have asked her to join, and we could have saved a wasted day for her.

The organizers of most strategic planning meetings want a diversity of participants who represent various stakeholders. Great goal, but incomplete. If I'm asked to facilitate the planning meeting, I ask how creative the people are attending. I suggest the organizers consider not inviting noncreative people. This surprises the organizer until I explain that a nonparticipating stakeholder is a waste of everyone's time, and I give them my example of Jessi. There are exceptions, of course; sometimes, noncreative people need to be included for company political reasons. Additionally, they may help mitigate risk by ensuring the plan is realistic. But everyone should be participative.

Who are your creative people? Who are your noncreative people? Which one are you? It is important that you recognize and use them strategically.

CHAPTER 5

Grower Innate Ability

"You have to believe it before you see it."
—Unknown

Growers are the innovators and entrepreneurs, although not all have or will start a business. It's the inventive innate ability that sets them apart from the other abilities. They typically don't like accountability and are creative, forward-thinking, and risk-takers. Proportionally, more people with ADHD can be found in the entrepreneur ranks than those with other abilities, which can be an asset to them. People in any position in the company can have the grower ability, but it is rarer than the other abilities. Some growers can spin idea after idea without ever implementing them or do so in a half-cocked fashion. The most successful ones also have some execution skills or the money to hire people who do.[1]

For several years, I taught an undergraduate entrepreneurship course. Somehow, I thought this class would attract budding business types with innovative new ideas—growers. I decided to take an informal survey of my students. To my surprise, most considered themselves chiefs followed by reckoners, implementors, growers, peddlers, then producers. Growers consistently came in third or fourth class after class, year after year. My students generally reflected society regardless of the course title. I shouldn't have been surprised. I concluded that a grower doesn't need to take a college course in entrepreneurship to become one; they will figure it out. They are growers after all. Classes in entrepreneurship teach the mechanics of employee management, basic marketing, business finance, return on investment, and how to evaluate a start-up.[2] They can't teach the innate ability of growers—innovating, recognizing opportunity, and creativity.

I have been friends with Maria for many years. We are the same age and grew up in the same town. She is the youngest of five children who lived in a rural area where the highest paying job was being a schoolteacher because the teachers could also run their farm after school and during the summer. Maria started working in a summer job as a low-paid assembly-line worker. She worked at a local camp trailer manufacturing company, one of two small industries in the community. The other one made fan belts for cars. Typical of the ability, Maria could not be repressed. She started working with a partner, Kelly, because their job, making the ceilings, required two workers to keep up with the assembly line.

Maria quickly got bored after mastering the job; it took her a week, so she figured out how to do the job faster and organize her work area more efficiently. She did so without informing her boss or asking permission; it made sense to her, so she did it. Through Maria's efforts, Kelly wasn't needed and was moved to another area of the assembly line. Kelly was fine with that because he didn't like ceilings.

With the changes Maria instituted, the ceiling station consistently worked way ahead of the production line. In fact, Maria could maintain that pace, working half the hours on ceilings. In short, she reduced the employee hours required for the ceiling station from 80 to 20, a 75 percent reduction. Her boss "rewarded" her by adding cleanup (fixing what was wrong before the trailers left the line) to her duties. Guess what happened there? Yep, she revolutionized cleanup, and another work partner was moved to another section. The changes Maria made continued after she left for her senior year of high school.

Maria went on to complete a master's degree in psychology because she was interested in human behavior, and it was the quickest path to get the "piece of paper." Many growers don't found companies, but Maria did. The companies she created, thirty-five years later, receive over a billion dollars annually in government contracts. She had no clue she would become a successful entrepreneur, but the grower signs were there, starting with her assembly-line job and each subsequent job until she took the leap of faith and started creating businesses.

It is easy to think of famous growers like Wolfgang Mozart, Elon Musk, Thomas Edison, Henry Ford, Mahatma Gandhi, Ben Franklin, and hundreds of others. J.K. Rowling,[3] author of the Harry Potter books, is one of them. On the surface, she seems an unlikely grower, certainly not in the typical entrepreneurial way. Rowling had a predilection for writing early, with her first book at six and a novel at eleven. She continued to write stories through primary and secondary education. At university, Rowling studied French and classics and continued to write as a hobby.

After graduating, Rowling worked as a secretary and researcher and wrote for fun. In 1990, while delayed on a train, Rowling formed the idea for Harry Potter and continued to jot ideas down on scraps of paper over the subsequent seven years. Also, in the early nineties, she experienced personal trials with her mother's death and a failed marriage. It was a dark time for her, yet she continued to write, planning seven Harry Potter novels. She finally completed the first manuscript and sent it to twelve publishers—who rejected it. A thirteenth publisher, Bloomsbury, picked it up, and the rest is history. In just twenty-three years after her first book was published, Rowling rose from a poor single mother to a billionaire.

Rowling was passionate about creative writing, starting early in life and continuing through good and bad times. Her wealth and success do not make her a grower, but her vision, dogged determination, and risking do. It is hard to repress a grower from doing what they do. They will figure out ways around rules and stretch boundaries like squeezing a balloon; putting pressure in one area expands other locations. Not all growers are successful; most start-ups fail. But others succeed, and virtually all were started by someone willing to take risks.

You can identify growers in your community. Who started the burger joint, clothing store, or dance studio? Who had a dream, mortgaged their house, or took out a loan to follow it? Others might not be so obvious; for example, the drama teacher who consistently produces novel high school plays or the police officer who organizes an inner-city basketball league for kids. Every composer, novelist, and choreographer possesses the grower ability, as do the assembly-line workers like Maria and thousands more who think, *Wait . . . what if we did it this way?*

You can find growers in every corporate position, but proportionately, more will be seen among the entrepreneurs and less among the accountants—you don't want an accountant who pushes the envelope; they are the ones you see on the news. A company without a grower may be stuck in the status quo much longer than needed. Growers simply see opportunities others don't and have innovative ideas others don't think about.[4]

Entrepreneurial growers tend to blur work and personal life. Most live to work, and many have a large financial and personal stake in whatever venture they have created. They work more hours than others and have a high achievement motivation. They are at greater risk for physical and emotional issues from the stress of financial risk, responsibility, and family conflict than others in executive positions, but most endure these while appearing self-confident.[5]

Those starting businesses wear multiple hats, including those they are not the best at, but their creativity gives them more flexibility in fulfilling various roles than the other innate abilities. Entrepreneurs, typically, must wear the hat of a salesperson to create a business if seeking financial backing, for example, or convincing others to implement a change within their existing company if they don't have the authority to make the changes themselves.[6]

CHAPTER 6

Chief Innate Ability

> "A leader is one who knows the way,
> goes the way, and shows the way."
> —John C. Maxwell

Chiefs are leaders. They take charge, and people naturally respect them. They develop instructions for others to follow. Their focus is on people rather than the process, and they are often charismatic.[1] The chief's ability is knowing how to achieve a goal and having the ability to identify and inspire other people to follow them to achieve it.[2] It is the most written about of the abilities. Search on Amazon or Barnes & Noble to see how many books deal with leadership.

When people think of leadership, they rightfully think of the C-Suite, political, religious, military, or sports leaders. Famous ones like Lee Iacocca, George MacArthur, Franklin D. Roosevelt, and John Wooden come to mind, as well as infamous ones like Adolph Hitler, Genghis Kahn, Jim Jones, and Joaquín Guzmán.

I like the story of one famous chief, Winston Churchill.[3] Much has been written about the man, and no one can deny he was the right leader at the right time for England. In brief, Churchill was born into an upper-class family but paid his dues by serving in the British military. He was a writer and inspirational orator who memorized all his speeches.

Churchill entered politics and served as a member of Parliament, eventually serving as the first lord of the admiralty but failed with the Gallipoli campaign and resigned. After fighting on the western front, he returned to Parliament and served as chancellor of the exchequer for five years but eventually lost his seat. After an eleven-year pause during which Churchill wrote and made speeches, he entered public office again and, following the resignation of Neville Chamberlain in 1940, was chosen to be the prime minister. And that is when things became interesting, and he went full stride as a chief. Churchill had the incredible task of leading Britain and the Allied powers to victory against the Nazis. Arguably, among his strengths was his power of oratory. He connected with the people of Great Britain, was called "the Bulldog," and inspired them with phrases like, "We will never surrender," "This was their finest hour," and "Never give in. Never give in. Never, never, never, never—in nothing, great or small, large or petty—never give in." You can imagine living at that time in England glued to your radio, knowing that disaster was around the corner and taking solace in your leader's words. Churchill was awarded the Nobel Prize for Literature and was the first to become an honorary US citizen.

Certainly, the chief innate ability is seen in famous historical figures, but it can be seen locally in ordinary people at all levels of a company. A classic example for me is Andreas. I have known and consulted with Andreas for about ten years. He impresses me every time I talk with him. At cocktail parties, he would be the one everyone would peg as some sort of boss at work. Andreas isn't the CEO, COO, or VP of anything, and interestingly, he doesn't want to be; however, Andreas embodies the innate ability of a chief. He is the oldest of nine children. His father was arrested for a series of thefts and sent to prison when Andreas was a young teenager. His parents divorced a few years later, and his mother became a nonfunctional parent.

Andreas assumed the leadership of the family. He didn't hesitate; the ability was in his blood. Almost two decades later, his siblings still go to him with issues, not their mother or now paroled father. Andreas joined the National Guard out of high school, worked as a diesel mechanic, and learned how to code. He had a knack for computer programming and landed a job as a software engineer. He was proficient in that role and quickly became an informal spokesman of the small cadre of fellow coders. His boss insightfully recognized Andreas's leadership potential and made him a department head of over ten engineers. After two years, he was bumped to the next level—division director—and became the boss of six department heads.

While he could do the other jobs, Andreas admits his replacements were better than he was. Those positions are better suited for people with producer and implementor abilities. The division director was the real match for Andreas's chief ability, and the company benefited from him in that position. He fired the dead wood, demoted those wrongfully advanced, and established clearer requirements for new hires. He assembled the right department heads, with complementary implementor abilities below him, giving them clear direction and precise goals.

Andreas could do good work in lower positions, but that's not the point. The abilities those jobs required were not his innate ability, and he found them exhausting. Once his job duties matched his chief innate ability, he took off, and work, while hard, was more pleasurable for him. The results were predictable because he and the people under him were working in the zone of their innate abilities. Andreas's division became the most productive in the company, and he is the recognized heir apparent for the CTO position in the company. Interestingly, he is not interested in it. He says he makes enough money and doesn't want to sacrifice the family time the CTO role would take from him. He also recognizes that a grower would best fill the CTO position, and he is not a grower. He doesn't want to be a statistic of the Peter principle. He clearly recognizes his innate chief ability and rightfully wants to stay in that zone. He also can temper the typical ladder-climbing temptation with his family values.

In his book, *Tribes*, Seth Godin asserts that anyone can be a leader; they just need to find a group to follow them.[4] The idea has some merit but doesn't get at the innate chief ability in leaders. Chiefs act on a vision or goal and assemble the team to bring it to fruition. When given something to undertake, a chief will think, *I'll have Susie do this, Mike do that, and Sabrina do the other thing.* They leave the details of how to accomplish their respective assignments to Susie, Mike, and Sabrina, especially if they have the implementor ability. Chiefs are intentional and committed for the long haul. They build relationships and are focused on the people needed to accomplish the objective. They are typically good coaches to others, and people develop loyalty to them, but they often need a grower to help create the vision.[5]

To illustrate, I committed five years to consult with a nonprofit whose initial offerings consisted of running a few twelve-step programs for men with pornography addictions. They also ran groups for the addicts' wives. The founders were a husband-and-wife team, Oliver and Emma. They were wonderful people who wanted to help couples struggling with the same issue as them. They ran most of the groups themselves, and Emma wrote a book about her experience with Oliver and his pornography addiction. They wanted to expand their reach.

Oliver and Emma are both chiefs. They were great at involving other people but couldn't see how to generate money and expand their offerings. Oliver and Emma had a few reckoners on their small board. My role was to be their grower. We hit upon several ideas while I worked with them. They started charging for the new offerings we created but kept the twelve-step programs free, something Oliver and Emma were insistent on. When my five-year commitment ended, they replaced me with a grower in the CEO position. The organization now runs hundreds of twelve-step programs and serves thousands of clients worldwide. They enjoy the revenue to have paid staff and are an excellent resource for the community.

Chiefs are the essential leaders to rally the troops to take care of business. They are the ones the employees look to and are inspired by. There is a reason so many business books are dedicated to leadership.

CHAPTER 7

Implementor Innate Ability

*"Management's job is to convey leadership's
message in a compelling and inspiring way."*
—Jeffery Gitomer

Implementors are the managers of tasks, an essential ability in successful organizations.[1] The critical distinction between them and chiefs is that implementors are focused on lining out the tasks to accomplish an objective, whereas chiefs are more focused on the people needed to achieve the outcome. Implementors are more focused on the process than the people. They have excellent execution skills.

It is a little difficult to identify historical implementors because chiefs and growers tend to get more press. Implementors are the right hands of presidents and dictators like Alexander Hamilton to George Washington and Nicols Sansenelli to Bento Mussolini, respectively. Talent managers like Janet Billig Rich and René Angélil and campaign managers like Brad Parscale are likely implementors. Part of the reason their work is concealed from the public eye is because the tasks of implementation are behind the scenes. No leader becomes great without good implementors behind them, making sure stuff gets done.

The competence of Jen O'Malley Dillon[2] struck me. Her first role in politics started by answering phones for the

Massachusetts attorney general. Later, O'Malley Dillon worked in various capacities for Al Gore's 2000 presidential campaign, the US Senate campaigns of Tim Johnson and Mary Landrieu, John Edwards's 2004 and 2008 presidential campaigns, Senator Tom Daschle's reelection campaigns, and Barack Obama's presidential campaign. After Obama's election, she worked on the presidential transition and then as director of the DNC under Tim Kaine. She worked on Obama's 2012 reelection campaign and later cofounded a political consulting firm that did work in the US and Canada and for US venture capital firms. O'Malley Dillon chaired the DNC's Unity Reform Commission and, in 2019, was instrumental in creating a data exchange that allowed for better information sharing between Democratic campaigns and allies. O'Malley Dillon became the manager of Beto O'Rourke's 2020 presidential campaign and later became the manager of Biden's 2020 presidential campaign. On November 16, 2020, O'Malley Dillon assumed the role of White House deputy chief of staff.

O'Malley Dillon has certainly had a wild, multipronged career to date. One can think that she is a chief, and indeed, she has had leadership roles, but her value is in her execution skills. That is why she is the go-to person for so many political leaders. They need a gifted implementor, which they found in Jen O'Malley Dillon.

Implementors tend to be more reserved than growers and chiefs and prefer to work for an established company with established procedures and practices. They thrive on clarity and dislike ambiguity. That was the biggest issue Susan, from the introduction, had with me and why she resigned. I failed to provide her with the direction she needed to be successful.

Implementors are good at envisioning goals and minimizing variables. Implementors develop methods that work for them and double down if their approach is threatened. They want to reduce risk but not as much as reckoners, who want no risk.

Implementors typically think in the short-term. They build systems and processes to be successful. When they delegate, they give precise assignments and are often more prescriptive on how to accomplish them than chiefs.[3]

An associate of mine, Sandra, told me about an epiphany she had regarding a man named Jarome. Sandra has known Jarome for several years. She met him when he was the VP of a small division of a regional home health company. Jarome was more than adequate in the role for the first few years. Sandra said Jarome did a superb job stabilizing the division after his predecessor was terminated for fraud. However, things changed when Jarome's boss challenged him to grow the division that had been stagnant for several years. Jarome was out of his element, which frustrated him and his boss. It often took Jarome too long to make decisions and plans. Sandra thought Jarome was competent and professional but too plodding for a leadership role. Jarome's excuse was that he didn't want to grow too fast and compromise the quality of the existing program. Under pressure, Jarome left the company to pursue other opportunities. Sandra wasn't surprised because she felt Jarome was not right for long-term leadership.

It's a small world, and after six years, Sandra discovered Jarome's other opportunity. He was the COO of a company Sandra had started consulting with. She attended a meeting of the executive leadership teams of the company she was consulting with and the company they were acquiring. The leadership of both companies was there. Sandra learned that days before the meeting, Jarome had compiled a list of things to do, people to meet with, offices to see, policies to review, and financial statements to examine. Most of the talking at the meeting came from the respective CEOs of the two companies. Jarome said very little during the meeting, only asking a few questions about things needing to be done for due diligence and nothing about people or their roles.

Sandra is familiar with the innate abilities and reflected, "At that meeting, the realization hit me like a ton of bricks; Jarome is a consummate implementor." Embarrassed by her misjudgment of Jarome, Sandra admitted she had made the same mistake many people make. She had judged Jarome's innate ability by his previous VP job title, wrongly associating that title with a correlated grower or chief ability. What Sandra thought was pedantic behavior years previously was Jarome doing what he does best, making sure systems were in place and functioning before moving forward. His innate ability was wasted in a grower or chief ability position. Sandra said Jarome demonstrated his implementor skills during the meeting and was in his zone. Jarome was the perfect complement to his CEO, who is a chief. It was the happiest and most proficient Sandra had ever seen Jarome.

Sandra had the opportunity to work more closely with Jarome after that group meeting. In the subsequent merging of the companies, Jarome oversaw all the details and tasks. He made sure none were missed. The merger was largely successful because of Jarome's excellent implementor skills.

It is not uncommon for implementors to end up leading small organizations. I have never seen one lead a large for-profit company that seems reserved for chiefs. I have seen dozens of nonprofit organizations led by implementors. In many cases, being an implementor works just fine, especially if the organization is already established and the status quo is to be maintained. It becomes a challenge if the organization needs to expand or change its offerings—not the strength of implementors.

I recently met with a group of building contractors. They were trying to run small construction businesses in addition to pounding nails. After spending a few hours with them, I could sense that they were implementors. They read the blueprints and executed the plans as designed in building houses. Most of them had a handful of employees who were all producers. They hired subcontractors—all producers—to complete their building projects as needed. The contractors were struggling to perform the other innate abilities' roles and not doing well at any of them. There wasn't a reckoner or chief in the bunch, for example. Some had their spouse keep the books, whether they had that ability or not. Interestingly, all had more work than they could do because of the building boom in the area, so a peddler and grower were not needed.

Just having implementor's and producer's innate abilities is typical of small construction companies and why many stay small. It is easy for them to reach the ceiling of complexity. Bringing on the other abilities would help to raise the ceiling, but many contractors are resistant because, as implementors, they have a hard time letting go of the details. The challenge is how to cover the other abilities so they can enjoy why they got into construction in the first place, which was likely not doing the office stuff. For many, one easy solution could be to contract with an accounting company to get at least the reckoner ability. Minimally, their books would be sound. Getting a chief on board would be more challenging; for some, hiring a construction foreman with the chief's ability could be a possible solution.

Interestingly, because business isn't suffering for this group, most were willing to do nothing and gut it out, having to perpetually emulate abilities they don't have. Many had done that for several years. They were excited at the prospect of retirement even though they were in their forties and fifties. They were exhausted consistently, up to their eyeballs. Had they been able to operate solely within their zone, they wouldn't be nearly as drained. They would also be better able to respond to a business downturn because having a complement of innate abilities can be employed strategically to increase their survival, as I outline in chapter 14.

I have a great appreciation for implementors. I get anxious

and overwhelmed when analyzing the steps needed to complete anything. As a grower, I have spent a whole career coming up with ideas and turning them over to implementors to make them happen.

CHAPTER 8

Reckoner Innate Ability

*"Behind every good business is
a great accountant."*
—Unknown

Reckoners are the rule followers. They are risk-averse and like everything in its place. Their offices and desks are typically neat and well-organized. This ability is the total opposite of the grower's ability.

I have known many reckoners in accounting positions in various companies, but they can thrive in other positions, such as HR professionals, editors, tech writers, attorneys, and judges. Reckoners generally keep a low profile, so finding one of note is challenging; however, two came to the public's attention in 2002. Accountants Cynthia Cooper and Sherron Watkins, who were among three women receiving *TIME* Magazine's Person of the Year that year.[1]

Cynthia Cooper[2] earned a bachelor's in accounting from Mississippi State University and a master's in accountancy from the University of Alabama. She is also a certified fraud examiner. Cooper worked for the public accounting firms PricewaterhouseCoopers and Deloitte & Touche in their Atlanta, GA, offices before becoming the VP of Internal Audit at Worldcom (now MCI, Inc.). There was a $3.8 billion fraud problem at

Worldcom that Cooper and her team stealthily uncovered—the largest corporate fraud in US history at the time.

After everything hit the fan, she continued to stay at Worldcom for two years to help the company emerge from bankruptcy. After Cooper left Worldcom, she created a consulting company and spoke with professionals and students about the lessons she had learned. She penned a book in 2008, *Extraordinary Circumstances: The Journey of a Corporate Whistleblower*, and donates the profits to high schools and universities for ethics education.

Sherron Watkins[3] received a bachelor's and master's degree in accounting from the University of Texas. She started her career in 1982 at Arthur Andersen as an auditor, spending the next eight years in their Houston and New York offices. She joined New York-based MG Trade Finance in 1990 with the role of managing their commodity-backed finance assets. In 1993, Watkins left to join Enron as their VP of corporate development.

In August 2001, Watkins alerted Kenneth Lay, Enron's then-CEO, of accounting irregularities in the company's financial reports. She was criticized by some for not reporting the fraud sooner to government authorities. Her memo regarding the fraud did not reach the public's attention until five months after she wrote it. She provided testimony before committees of the US House of Representatives and Senate at the beginning of 2002 regarding her unheeded warnings to Lay. Enron filed for bankruptcy in December 2001 and ceased operations in 2007.

When the dust settled, Watkins started giving speeches at colleges and management groups. She wrote a book about her Enron experiences and what she sees as problems with US corporate culture. It's called *Power Failure: The Inside Story of the Collapse of Enron*.

What makes Cooper and Watkins reckoners? The fact that both graduated in accounting and were CPAs is a big clue. The reckoner innate ability is closely allied with accountants. In addition, they respectfully paid attention to the details and rules to identify fraudulent practices at Worldcom and Enron. They didn't gloss over the signs as people with some of the other innate abilities might have done. To their credit, Cooper and Watkins had the courage to speak up about the fraud. They knew they were right and weren't afraid to broadcast it.

I had my own experience with fraud many years ago. At the time, my company had two bookkeepers, a newly hired accountant, Allie, and Brad, who had been on board a little over a year and was the boss of the shop. Brad was embezzling funds. A little here, a little there. The two bookkeepers were suspicious that something was off, but they couldn't put their finger on it. They informed Allie, who dug into the issue. She reviewed several months of transactions, bills, receipts, and payments. Allie discovered what Brad was doing, how he was doing it, and how much had been misappropriated—a little over $30,000. In her investigation, Allie also discovered that Brad had never graduated in accounting and, in fact, had never attended college. He was a fake. Allie alerted me, and I called the cops. I got to help the white-collar fraud division investigate Brad. I even wore a wire during one-on-one meetings with him. I felt like 007. On the strength of Allie's fact-finding and clear documentation, Brad was arrested. He had no priors and was able to plea out of jail time. My company was fortunate it only lost $30,000. Who knows? If left undiscovered, Brad may have embezzled much more.

Another reckoner I am grateful for is Adrian. She was the youngest of three children, growing up in a large metropolitan area in the western US. Sadly, that is all I know about her. She only talked about work at work, and we never socialized. Adrian was very predictable; she arrived at work at precisely 8 a.m. and left at 5 p.m., lunch consistently from 12 to 12:30 p.m., and she always brought it from home. People in the office joked that you could set your watch by Adrian's adherence to routine. Adrian thrived on the repetitive, possibly because she didn't have to think about it. She maintained a hard copy of everything, yet, despite that, her office and desk were free from clutter. She could find anything in an instant because of the filing system she established. She was a good accountant, and the company's books were in great hands with Adrian.

She had no idea why I would be interested in expanding the company into another state and warned me that it was costing the company too much money. She saw that as risky. She was right, of course, but she didn't recognize the up potential because it was too abstract. Ultimately, however, that expansion state eventually became the company's largest and most profitable operation.

I was invited to educate various groups of people on the company's offerings in a New England state. I rented a car from Hertz with a NeverLost navigation system (maps on a cell phone weren't a thing back then), and Adrian was my passenger. She brought a road map and was consulting it from time to time. She continued reading the map even after I told her the GPS was guiding us. She said she didn't trust it. She consulted the map, validating the GPS with each city we visited. At the end of the multiday trip, Adrian said, "Well, I guess that thing did work after all."

At her retirement party I got to meet her two daughters and husband for the first time. She stood at the appropriate moment; I am sure the room, like me, was waiting with bated breath to hear what she would say. She said, "I enjoyed working for the company. I will enjoy retirement. Thanks to you all for coming," and sat down. That was it. I thought, *So Adrian*.

Most reckoners don't have Adrian's quirks, but as a group, they are the most homogeneous of the abilities. To illustrate, despite trying to recruit students with a broader range of traits for eight years, Kansas State University failed to attract more diverse students to their accounting classes. The classes apparently only appealed to people with the reckoner innate ability. This ability is found more than twice as often in accountants than in other positions.[4]

Reckoners are often empathetic, conscientious, and ethical. They are often less open, less agreeable, and less assertive than non-reckoners. They are typically not entrepreneurial or extroverted. They pay attention to detail, have excellent math skills, and have a good working knowledge of best practices.[5] Some joke that reckoners have their personality removed in accounting school; that is a stereotype that is not true, but few are the life of the party.

I have learned to appreciate the ability of reckoners. As a grower, I have been guilty of considering them a necessary evil, anchors preventing me from implementing my great ideas. In truth, they are the foundation, stabilizing the proverbial ship so we don't sink, an innate ability essential to any successful long-term business.

CHAPTER 9

Peddler Innate Ability

> "Buyers don't believe anything you have to say to them about your product or service until they first believe in you."
> —Deb Calvert

Peddlers are often charming, confident, and likable. They are goal-oriented, assertive, sympathetic, and persistent. The most successful ones are customer-centered, not easily discouraged, modest, conscientious, and curious, and they have great communication skills.[1]

What good is making a product or providing a service if no one knows about it? That's where the peddlers come in. Peddlers are the salespeople. Some examples of the most extraordinary peddlers from history include David Ogilvy, Ron Popeil, Mary Kay Ash, and Billy Mays. There are some infamous ones as well, including Charles Ponzi and Bernie Madoff. Peddlers can inspire you to buy what they are selling. They are the ones who proactively broadcast the good news of the company regardless of their position in the company.

One famous peddler is Erica Feidner.[2] Feidner grew up in Vermont in a family of seven, with twenty-six pianos. Her family ran a piano camp each summer that would host forty children from around the world, which exposed Feidner to different cultures.

She started playing piano at three and became an instructor at nine. Feidner was awarded a scholarship to Juilliard Prep at ten and made the five-hour commute from her home to Juilliard every weekend by herself. At eleven, she made her first solo orchestral debut. In college, she saw an ad for the Miss America pageant, and, wanting to earn the prize so she could buy a better piano, Feidner decided to enter. She was crowned Miss Vermont and later won the talent award in the Miss America pageant.

While skiing, Feidner injured her hand so severely that it ended her dreams of becoming a concert pianist, so she decided to get an MBA. She eventually landed a job working for Steinway, where her peddler ability kicked in. Feidner became the top salesperson in the entire company. In just eight years, she sold an unfathomable number of pianos, $41-million worth, and was given the nickname "The Piano Matchmaker." What made Feidner such a great salesperson? There are several reasons, but her expertise as a player was certainly top among them. She was also friendly, engaging, and charming and believed in her product. Feidner attributed her success to taking the time to clearly explain what the customer needed to know to understand Steinway pianos. She stated, "If you cannot tell the difference and thus know which piano is right for you, I haven't yet succeeded."

Feidner became famous worldwide for her sales prowess, so much so that she has coached top executives in Fortune 500 companies. Now retired from Steinway, she hawks a piano method she invented to help students have fun while learning to play the piano. Feidner also gives private and group piano lessons in person or virtually.

Over the years, in the nonprofit business, I have been frustrated by the lack of peddlers. My organization supports people with disabilities. The terrific quality of our services is the biggest secret in town. Everyone works with their heads down and does not think to advertise the good outcomes they are achieving, something a peddler would naturally do. Peddlers see opportunities to find new customers and ways to cultivate existing ones.[3] They are passionate about what they are selling, whether that enthusiasm is genuine or not. They are often extroverts, cheerful, seek excitement, and like people and large groups.[4]

While many peddlers go into sales, the ability is broader. My nonprofit company does not employ a salesforce; rather, it depends on each location creating and maintaining good relationships with our government-funding partners. The employee who demonstrates the peddler ability, if there is one, should be the point person. Most of my employees are implementors and producers, and they assume if they do well, the funders will notice. They don't. Peddlers don't wait to be noticed; they will say, "Hey, come see the great things the company is doing."

The best peddler my company hired was Nikki. She was smooth and likable. Nikki wasn't hired as a salesperson but rather as an executive over one of the stagnant company's divisions. She catered to funders and her employees. Everyone loved her, and she grew services like crazy. Everyone believed her because what she said was so believable. I enjoyed hanging out with Nikki. She was a lot of fun. From a growth standpoint, she was very beneficial to her division—unfortunately, not from a credibility perspective. She couldn't actually deliver much of what she promised. Quickly, as her bosses started pinning her down and asking the right questions, she resigned and was gone within days. Nikki had a character flaw that marred a brilliant, innate peddler ability.

The story of Amini illustrates another peddler example. I have known Amini for over forty years. He came very premature into this world, weighing less than two pounds. He credits his grandmother for his survival because of her constant vigilance. He grew up in a single-parent household with his two sisters in a

US, Mexico border city. Amini kept under the radar in the public school system, avoiding gang involvement and keeping his nose clean. He joined the army as quickly as he could and served a stint in Germany. After his military service, Amini went to college on the GI bill, earning an undergraduate degree in sociology. He landed a job in finance after graduation. His specialty was selling high-risk loans to people living in economically challenged neighborhoods in a large West Coast city. He was very successful but felt guilty with each loan. Amini thought the bank took advantage of its customers, charging exorbitant fees and justifying them because of the client's low credit ratings. He was relieved when he could finally retire. Amini wanted to serve his community and became a volunteer with the metropolitan police force, serving as a chaplain. He has also volunteered for several years as the regional coordinator of the Just Serve[5] program, interacting with various faith-based communities and providing volunteer service projects throughout the county. Amini has never been busier or happier. He is in his element. His peddler ability is what made him successful as a financial adviser. It is also critical in his role as chaplain, where he helps families figure out other options for their lives. In addition, his peddler ability is essential in winning the trust of various community and church leaders and helping hundreds of volunteers work together for the greater good.

He and his wife could not have children, but he has become a father and grandfather figure to many families in his church and officers on the police force. Amini is so humble and genuine that you believe he is your friend; you probably are. Charming and personable, I have never met anyone who doesn't like him.

Growers can look like peddlers when trying to promote their ideas. What is the difference between them? Using other terms, is an entrepreneur similar to a salesperson? There is overlap in the marketing of ideas to influence others. The key difference is the personal risk and consistent production of novel ideas. In addition, peddlers are typically more socially savvy than growers.

As a group, peddlers often get a bum rap. Everyone can tell stories of the disingenuous car salesperson or their uncle, the insurance guy. Granted, some salespeople earn the reputation, like the young man trying to sell me solar panels. He couldn't imagine why I wasn't interested, even after I showed him how it would take me twenty years to break even, and by then, the panels would have to be replaced. He kept pushing until I almost politely shut the door in his face.

Thank goodness for peddlers. Promotion is the lifeblood of any business, whether tech, cars, or nonprofits. Someone has to get out there and sell what the company is offering. Without them, businesses won't get very far.

CHAPTER 10

Producer Innate Ability

"I can make a General in five minutes but a
good horse is hard to replace."
—Abraham Lincoln

Producers are the workers. Many want to do their job and go home. Performing tasks that the company gets paid for is their work product. Producers are not lazy or without talent, ability, and ambition. They don't go around with their heads down. Their values and priorities are outside of work. They generally like some upward mobility as long as it doesn't push them too much out of their comfort zone.

It is challenging to identify famous producers. However, thanks to internet searches, a few have made headlines because of their surprising wealth discovered after they died, including Margaret Southern, a schoolteacher, and Ronald Read, a janitor. They were content to live frugally, plowing what they could as buy and hold investments into conservative stocks and accumulating millions. One who caught my attention was Sylvia Bloom.[1]

Bloom was a secretary in the Manhattan law firm Cleary Gottlieb Steen & Hamilton until she retired at ninety-six. She outlived her husband by a couple of decades. He was likely a producer as well, working as a fireman and later as a schoolteacher before he retired. Sylvia dutifully took the subway to work and back each day for sixty-seven years, except when the World Trade Center was attacked. It was said that she retired so she could work on her bridge game, a pastime she enjoyed immensely.

Bloom lived an unassuming, unremarkable life in her one-bedroom Brooklyn apartment. When she died at ninety-seven, she left $6.24 million to the Henry Street Settlement, a social services organization located on the Lower East Side of Manhattan, and $2 million to Hunter College, her alma mater. Neither her family nor her closest friends knew of Bloom's wealth.

If Bloom was a producer, how did she amass such wealth? Turns out that one of her tasks as a secretary was to place investments for the lawyers. Her investment strategy was to buy a few shares of the same stock her boss bought, although her income tempered the amount Bloom could buy. Notice that none of the firm's attorneys have made the papers for the millions they left behind.

The approach of producers was exemplified to me a short time ago. I met with one of the owners of a company that operates a chain of several auto repair shops. The owners are retiring and, believing they have enough money, wanted to gift company ownership to the mechanics who have worked so hard for them over the years. Over lunch one day, Steve, the person charged with communicating the plan, told me how excited he was to make the announcement. He was confident the employees would be elated and applaud the big news. They would have an equity stake in the company, with no out-of-pocket money. But, to Steve's shock and dismay, there was no clapping or cheering. The mechanics were, at best, lukewarm to the prospect. Most were just not interested. They wanted to "turn wrench" from nine-to-five and go home. They didn't want the hassle of what ownership of the company would require. Creating an employee-owned company was dead on arrival because the company employed producers who were not that invested, even after working there for years.

Producers are essential to every business. Producers are everywhere, from entry-level to executive positions. Being a producer is an underrated ability and one that should be acknowledged. People with the producer ability deliver our mail, make our cars, and serve our food. You find them among teachers, software engineers, mechanics, accountants, farmers, clergy, lawyers, and journalists. In short, they are at the heart of every industry, but don't expect a producer to be anything other than a producer.

To illustrate, an acquaintance of mine, Jeremy, told me of an unfortunate experience he had. Jeremy is a licensed building contractor and successful entrepreneur, a grower. He said he had a great idea, or so he thought at the time, of creating a handyperson franchise. He was inspired by the example of Rent A Husband[2] and thought he could capitalize on the same customer base of people who are not handy themselves and couldn't get a contractor to do small, odd jobs. Jeremy approached Bill, a friend who had a business making cabinets. Bill liked the idea. In truth, Bill just wanted a change of jobs even though he owned the business, but Jeremy didn't know that then.

Jeremy and Bill met repeatedly to plan the business. Jeremy bankrolled the enterprise. He hired a designer to create the logo and initial marketing materials and a law firm to register the service mark and create the franchise documents. Jeremy placed ads in a national franchising magazine. Jeremy also spent hours creating the franchise manual, something Bill was supposed to do but never got around to. Bill did become the prototype franchisee, a role he was comfortable with—until he got tired of it after a couple of years. Typical of a grower, Jeremy was all in. He spent his savings of $250,000 on getting the company to that point and had the epiphany that another $250,000 was needed to get the word out there. Because they were equal partners,

Jeremy met with Bill to see what money Bill had to chip in. Bill said he couldn't help because he just bought a boat. Jeremy told me he was stunned. "How could Bill buy a boat when we needed money to get the business going?" Jeremy realized for the first time that Bill's level of commitment was totally different from his. He said, "I was willing to spend my savings creating that business, but Bill was more interested in boating."

I told Jeremy about the innate abilities and explained the disconnect. I said that he was a grower and Bill was a producer. Bill was interested in participating in the discussions and giving input, but he wasn't all that personally invested in the venture. At the outset, had Jeremy known that Bill was a producer, Jeremy would have had different expectations. Jeremy made a classic mistake that others were just like him. In retrospect, it is easy to see that Bill was not.

Out of money to advertise to attract franchisees, the business folded, and the two friends became estranged. Bill went to work for a big-box home improvement store and, every couple of years or so, reaches out to Jeremy for a job.

Producers aren't just laborers. Many professionals are producers; Naka is an example. She was an excellent behavioral health specialist, with a stellar reputation, who came to work for us from the state. She worked at one of my organization's behavioral intensive residential programs. Her real love was hiking, camping, and boating with her wife and their two Labradors. Years ago, the director encouraged Naka to replace him after he moved to pursue another opportunity. At the time, Naka was interested because it paid $15,000 more than her current position, and she was complimented that the director recommended her. When the time came, we offered Naka the position, and she accepted. The staff were excited and felt Naka was the logical person for the job. After two months, she requested to go back to her previous position. She hated being a supervisor.

Naka was perfectly content to work her shift and go home. Although her work was often stressful, it was predictable, and she didn't have to worry about supervising others. The director's job wasn't worth the money and interfered with her outdoor activities. Luckily, Naka recognized her innate ability mismatch with the job requirements. She requested a demotion rather than being miserable, quitting, or failing. She worked several more years before retiring.

My favorite producer story is Willy. He was a WWII vet. When he came home from the war, he met Florence, and the two fell in love. Florence had two kids from a previous marriage, so Willy quickly got a job at the nearby steel mill to support the family. He ended up working on the same machine, doing the same job for thirty years. Willy loved his family and large garden and orchard, spending all his time with his family or raising food. He was deeply religious and did a fair amount of humanitarian work through his church when the kids moved out.

I never saw Willy without a smile. He was the happiest person I ever met, a real joy to be around. I was curious why he never complained. He would literally whistle to work and whistle home again. After he retired, I asked Willy if he ever got bored at work. He said he didn't think about it that way, saying, "When I got back from the war, I had no schooling and a new family to feed. I needed a job, and the steel mill was the highest paying one I could get." Then he said something that caught me off guard. "I just decided to be happy about it." I was operating under the perspective that if a job didn't make you happy, change jobs. His philosophy was if a job didn't make you happy, change your attitude. It was then that I realized Willy worked to live, not lived to work. That doesn't mean Willy didn't seek every opportunity he could to work overtime. Producers can be very hardworking, and many work long hours. The point is they typically don't live for their job. In Willy's case, he balanced family time with the need for extra money when working extra hours as opposed to a love for the job. Life for Willy, his joys and rewards, was at home; the job was just a mechanism to pay the bills.

There are hundreds of books on career mobility and how to foster management and leadership among employees. There are no books about celebrating the innate ability of a producer, people who are satisfied where they are and whose lives exist outside of work. Business and self-help books are based on the premise that people want to advance up the corporate ladder. While that is true for many, there are many more who don't want the stress of a higher position; they are happy where they are. And in truth, aren't we glad?

CHAPTER 11

Identifying the Innate Abilities

*"The way to get started is to quit talking
and begin doing."*
—Walt Disney

There are many outward signs of the innate abilities and fuzzy distinctions between them, as seen in figure 1 in chapter 4. People can wear different hats of the abilities and get by—most of us do—but it isn't their default. This chapter aims to help you identify the innate ability of yourself and your coworkers.

There isn't a test out there that can diagnose them accurately, and even if there were, it would be suspect. The Kolby A[1] comes the closest; while thousands have taken it, there is scant research to back its claims. As I discussed in chapter 3, the Myers-Briggs and Big Five supposedly identify personality differences, but they aren't the same as innate abilities. The best way to identify innate abilities is through listening and observing.

It's time for you to identify the innate ability of your team. Listed below are ten traits typical of the abilities as observed by me and others.[2] Write your or a member of your team's name in the area provided. You can list multiple people on a line. You can leave a line blank if you have no one who fits the description. If you have someone who seems to fit multiple categories, think about where they would place themselves as a tiebreaker.

Grower—the person who mortgages their home to buy a mountain.

1. Focused on novel ideas.
2. High-risk tolerant.
3. Often creative.
4. Are competitive.
5. High tolerance for ambiguity.
6. Energized by new prospects.
7. See opportunities where others don't.
8. See the forest, not the trees.
9. Can be extroverts when needed.
10. High internal locus of control.

Who on your team has this innate ability?
_____

Chief—the person who organizes a team to climb the mountain.

1. Focused on the people needed to accomplish the objective.
2. Medium- to high-risk tolerant.
3. Create a vision for others.
4. Good at coaching and mentoring.
5. Are change agents.
6. Comfortable in their own shoes.
7. Willing to try new things.
8. Are long-term oriented.
9. Influence the process.
10. Understand a team is more effective than individuals.

Who on your team has this innate ability?
_____

Implementor—the person who ensures everyone packs a lunch on the hike.

1. Focused on lining out the tasks to accomplish the objective.
2. Medium- to low-risk tolerant.
3. Need an established vision.
4. Are good at organizing.
5. Are process-oriented.
6. Control various aspects of projects.
7. Do not look for opportunities.
8. Think short-term.
9. Rely on existing, proven skills.
10. Work best with established procedures and practices.

Who on your team has this innate ability?
_____

Reckoner—the person who brings a map to ensure the group follows the right trail.

1. Focused on rules and accountability.
2. Low-risk tolerance.
3. Good problem-solving skills.
4. Are organized and orderly.
5. Implement strategies developed by others.
6. Dislike expansion.
7. Have a clear set of standards they want followed.
8. Get things done in the most efficient way possible.
9. Have excellent attention to detail.
10. Work toward task completion regardless of distractions.

Who on your team has this innate ability?
_____

Peddler—the person who sells the movie rights to the experience.

1. Focused on promoting the company's offerings.
2. Medium- to high-risk tolerant.
3. Enjoy competition.
4. Achievement-oriented.
5. Friendly and likable.
6. Assertive.
7. Have high emotional intelligence.
8. Can be tenacious.
9. Are often charming.
10. Are typically extroverts.

Who on your team has this innate ability?
_____

Producer—the person who carries everyone else's water.

1. Focused on doing the work.
2. Medium- to low-risk tolerance.
3. Focused energy on the job at hand.
4. Concrete thinkers.
5. Low tolerance for ambiguity.
6. Do not aspire to leadership positions.
7. Separate work and personal life.
8. Have a variety of skill sets.
9. Work to live.
10. Want clear job expectations.

Who on your team has this innate ability?
_____

Were you able to identify the innate abilities of yourself and your teammates? Were there any surprises? How easy was it? Were there multiple people in one or more categories and none in others? Knowing this information is a critical first step. Knowing what to look for can help whoever is hiring or promoting to select the right person, which will be discussed in detail in the next chapters.

CHAPTER 12

Individual Differences

"Every individual matters.
Every individual has a role to play.
Every individual makes a difference."
—Jane Goodall

I am often asked about individual differences. I am a grower, and so are Sir Richard Branson and Eric Dowdle. I founded a couple of successful companies and a couple that failed. I am reserved and dislike attention and groups of people. Branson is a world-famous entrepreneur, billionaire, and adventurer. Documentaries have been made on him. Dowdle is a friend of mine, an artist, and a successful picture jigsaw puzzle maker. He has made a couple of TV series and has a fun and larger-than-life personality. Although Branson, Dowdle, and I are growers, we have a world of difference.

Every grower, chief, implementor, reckoner, peddler, and producer differs from others, even though they have the same innate ability. In figure 1, chapter 4, I show a range and overlap of the abilities. People with each ability exist on a spectrum, having varying degrees of the ability. The overlap of the abilities depicted in figure 1 also shows how the abilities aren't necessarily singular. People can be a combination of a few or at least emulate them successfully. In addition, people have different personalities that the personality tests I maligned previously strive to explain.

I have met and worked with people of various ages, races, faiths, and sexes in many countries, both hemispheres, and from north and south of the equator. The innate abilities transcend these differences and are universal human traits. There are, however, differences in the culture surrounding them and how they are exhibited. For example, I currently work with Hadia and Nohj, directors of separate orphanages in Uganda. My goal for them is to create a mechanism whereby they can generate revenue and become less dependent on donations. Without visiting the orphanages, I devised plans for each, including raising their own food and making swag to sell to tourists. When I explained my ideas to Hadia and Nohj, they were supportive and positive. I thought I was a genius. When I visited their orphanages, I realized my "solution" was stupid. They didn't have enough water or laborers to raise the crops, and no tourists visited them to buy anything. Semi-exasperated, I asked Hadia and Nohj if they had any ideas on self-sufficiency. They did and already had plans drawn up, sitting in their desks. They were great ideas. It was only then that I realized Hadia and Nohj were growers. Their culture taught them to be subservient to me and not volunteer information unless asked. They don't act like typical American growers; they act like typical Ugandan growers. The innate ability is the same, but the Ugandan culture affects how it is manifested.

Deb O'Dell, a dear departed friend of mine, once quipped, "People are messy." So true. Just think of the different labels out there that try and explain human behavior: are you a type A or B person, left-brained or right-brained, an extrovert or an introvert? If you are young, Cattell says you have more fluid intelligence, and if you are old, you have more crystallized intelligence.[1] In addition, we've learned that people have different personality characteristics; some are passive, others aggressive. We understand that people have different ways of learning; some are visual, others auditory or kinesthetic. We learn from Gardner that people also possess different intelligence levels and kinds.[2] Behavioral health comes into play; some people have ADHD, are on the autism spectrum, have depression, are bipolar, or have an anxiety or personality disorder. Many people have experienced severe trauma in their lives, including repression and discrimination, that impacts them. Add personal levels of honesty, trustworthiness, friendliness, and morality, and people paint a complicated picture indeed.

Hiring is challenging because you are dealing with all those complexities. Understanding people can seem overwhelming—because it is, and you can't control any of it. What you can control is hiring with innate abilities in mind. You can narrow the applicant pool to people with the innate ability you need, which will increase your chances of hiring the right candidate.

What happens when you need to hire a reckoner for an HR position and end up with three equally qualified reckoner applicants? You hire the one you like best. If, on the other hand, you have a similarly suitable reckoner, chief, and grower apply, your first choice should be the reckoner because that is the ability you need. What if you don't like the reckoner applicant for whatever reason? Rather than hiring the chief or grower as a fallback, if you have the luxury, you should consider rerunning the job ad; otherwise, you will repeat what hasn't worked for you in the past and end up with a job ability requirement and employee ability mismatch. Now comes the leap of faith. What if you like the reckoner, but their experience or education is anemic? Consider hiring them anyway and providing them the training they lack. You can't create the innate ability you need through education, but you can teach a person to do a job. Your goal in hiring is to find the person with the right innate ability who also adequately fits the other requirements of whatever position you are hiring for.

Consider Sir Isaac Newton.[3] After a thirty-five-year career as a physicist and professor (what we read about in the history books), in 1696, he was appointed warden of the British Royal Mint (what we don't read about). We can't know precisely why Charles Montague, chancellor of the exchequer, endorsed him for this position, but let's examine what the Mint needed. At that time, the Mint had silver coins in circulation that were worth less than the silver they were made of, and some of them were over 100 years old. They also needed to exchange Scotland's money for the Crown's. In addition, they had a massive problem with counterfeiters. These problems required out-of-the-box thinking; they required a grower.

Imagine you were interviewing Newton for the job. He knew little about coinage or economics and had no education or experience in law enforcement. He had never investigated, prosecuted, or imprisoned anyone. Would you hire him? He was not qualified for the job on paper, but if you paid attention in the interview, you would learn he was a crucial figure in the Scientific Revolution. He wrote a pioneering book, *Philosophiæ Naturalis Principia Mathematica*, made groundbreaking contributions to optics, and worked with another mathematician to develop infinitesimal calculus. Newton was a grower whom the Mint hired, perhaps in a leap of faith.

So, how did he do as warden, then master of the Mint? While he didn't change the Mint or its operations in the thirty-one years he worked there—it was a bureaucracy, after all—he was successful, comparable to his contributions to physics and mathematics. He accomplished the recoinage of England's currency in three years. He got Scotland's money exchanged for the Crown's and argued ahead of his time for paper money as an alternative to precious metals. He also focused on the counterfeiters. He investigated and brought numerous slick and savvy criminals to justice over the subsequent years. I mean, really, can you imagine being a criminal in the day knowing that arguably the smartest man alive was on your tail? Newton used his grower ability to do the things that needed creativity. He was eventually knighted largely because of his work at the Mint. His grower ability was more important for the Mint at that time than relevant education or experience.

CHAPTER 13

Innate Ability Hiring

"The most effective way to do it is to do it."
—Amelia Earhart

Many jobs have role descriptions that must be met, as well as education, specialized training, licenses, certificates, or experience. I am not advocating you throw those out. Keep them.

Some companies require applicants to take a personality test like the Myers-Briggs, Big Five, Kolbe A, or Color Code.[1] You can certainly continue using those; just don't base personnel decisions on them. Their results should only be considered fun and interesting. Despite their common usage, they are personality tests, not designed to determine goodness of fit for a position you are hiring for.

Other companies use hiring agencies or "headhunters." Their promotional materials promise great results. If that is your practice, please continue using them. I have seen good hires and bad hires using headhunters. They are great at identifying people with the specific professional credentials you are looking for in executive positions, for example.

You don't need to change how your company currently hires, but add screening for innate abilities to your hiring protocol. That simple addition will increase your chances of hiring the right person or avoiding the Peter principle if promoting internally more than anything else you do. It will certainly be more predictive than personality tests, references, letters of recommendation, or the content of résumés. It will require you to apply the art of listening in a different way during the interview process.

In chapter 11, you listed the people on your team that fit in each ability. Do you have any abilities missing names? Do you have more names in certain abilities than others?

Now, imagine you have an opening; the job title or position don't matter since a balanced team will have at least one person with each innate ability. You need to hire someone that fills the ability hole in your team. That is the person you need to identify in the hiring process.

But what if there are only two of you? You will automatically have blanks. Reconsider the previous exercise and write the person's name next to their primary ability and again in a second or third ability, labeling them correspondingly or indicating they are emulating that ability. Don't lose sleep over this; write your first thoughts. It shouldn't take more than a few minutes to do this. Your first impression will be the most accurate. The idea is to identify holes quickly. If you are building your team, subsequent hires should eliminate all the secondary and emulated abilities. The goal is to build a team that complements each other regardless of their job title. If you stay a team of two, you will know each other's lanes and not cross over roles.

Even if you have a team with all the innate abilities present, other factors can come into play. You can't control, for example, if a team member starts abusing drugs or alcohol or if physical or mental health issues occur. You won't be able to predict who might turn out to be a criminal (I've hired a few). But those challenges are your reality now. Innate ability hiring won't alter that. It will increase your odds of getting the right people in the right seat in your company.

But how do you do it? It is actually simpler than it seems. You pay attention to the cues people give off when they describe themselves and their past efforts. You have to listen with the abilities in mind. The more you listen for them, the easier it is to spot them. Continue to ask your standard interview questions and pay attention to how a candidate answers. To illustrate, I have given sample answers to some typical interview questions:[2]

1. Tell me something about yourself that isn't on your résumé.
    Grower—*I am constantly coming up with new ideas.*
    Chief—*I organized participants for a fundraising event.*
    Implementor—*I am a very detailed person.*
    Reckoner—*I am a neat freak. I love to keep things organized.*
    Peddler—*I sold pest control products for three summers.*
    Producer—*I enjoy outdoor sports.*
2. Where do you see yourself in five years?
    Grower—*In five years, I want to own my own business.*
    Chief—*I would like to develop ways to help employees work more efficiently.*
    Implementor—*I would like to earn my Lean Six Sigma certification.*
    Reckoner—*I would like to renew my CPA license and apply for a CFO position in the company if it becomes available.*
    Peddler—*I would like to get my real estate license.*
    Producer—*To be honest, I just want job stability. I hope to be happy in this position.*
3. How would other people describe you?
    Grower—*That I am good at seeing opportunities for expansion.*

Chief—*That I am a leader; people follow me.*
Implementor—*That I get things done.*
Reckoner—*That I am great at math and problem-solving.*
Peddler—*That I am a people person.*
Producer—*That I am loyal.*

4. What motivates you?
   Grower—*Brainstorming with idea partners.*
   Chief—*A well-functioning team.*
   Implementor—*Figuring out how to accomplish something.*
   Reckoner—*Having undisturbed time to figure something out.*
   Peddler—*Explaining a new concept to others.*
   Producer—*Having time with my family.*

5. What are you most passionate about?
   Grower—*New ideas.*
   Chief—*Helping people achieve.*
   Implementor—*Accomplishing goals.*
   Reckoner—*Providing information leaders need to make smart decisions.*
   Peddler—*Helping people understand the benefits of our service.*
   Producer—*Doing volunteer work at the local soup kitchen.*

6. What are your weaknesses?
   Grower—*I have a hard time with people who don't see the vision.*
   Chief—*Being too trustworthy of others.*
   Implementor—*Sometimes, I spend too much time planning what needs to be done rather than diving right in.*

Reckoner—*Sometimes, I have a hard time working with others.*
Peddler—*I lack patience.*
Producer—*Sometimes, I get bored with the routine of my job.*

7. What are your strengths?
Grower—*I'm the idea person on the team. I am good at out-of-the-box thinking.*
Chief—*I have never held a job where I sat in a starting position. I am quickly advanced into a boss position. And I am really comfortable leading a team.*
Implementor—*Last year, management handed down a strategic plan without any thought about how we were going to do it. I was able to create the implementation plan.*
Reckoner—*One of my biggest strengths is that I am doggedly determined. I will keep at something until it is accomplished.*
Peddler—*Other people have told me that I am funny and inspirational.*
Producer—*I love my job and am good at it. I believe that is a strength.*

8. Give an example of how you solved a problem in the past.
Grower—*I figured out another way of approaching the situation, and it worked out great.*
Chief—*By forming a team to generate solutions.*
Implementor—*I was able to implement a strategy that worked for me in the past.*
Reckoner—*I took the time to analyze the situation and bounced it off management to get their buy-in and they successfully moved it forward.*
Peddler—*The company was losing market share and I developed a social media campaign that*

management bought into.

Producer—*No one on the floor understood how to implement a new procedure. I met with my boss and explained the issue; she finally understood what we had been complaining about. She instituted more training, and things improved dramatically.*

9. What do you consider your best accomplishment in your last job?

    Grower—*I had a great idea about offering a new service. It was very well received.*

    Chief—*I was able to develop a strategic plan around a new product launch, and it was the best in the company's history.*

    Implementor—*I got to plan the whole implementation strategy for a new product rollout.*

    Reckoner—*I was finally able to create a four year-over-year cost analysis and showed where the company was bleeding. Management acted, and the company saved $563,000 in six months.*

    Peddler—*I was able to design the media marketing campaign for the company's new service line.*

    Producer—*I was able to point out problems with the company's documentation procedure that were causing overtime.*

10. Think about something you consider a work failure in your life, and tell me why you think it happened.

    Grower—*Early in my career, I had to work on an assembly line. I had a lot of ideas on how to make things better. No one cared, so I quit.*

    Chief—*In my last job, I assumed leadership of an existing team. They had a lot of deadwood, and I wasn't allowed to fire or reassign anyone. It was impossible.*

Implementor—*I was given an assignment but no training or instruction. I had no idea how to do what they were asking me to do.*

Reckoner—*I discovered some unethical practices. I pointed them out to those involved as kindly as I could. They got defensive and dismissed my concerns.*

Peddler—*I just couldn't get motivated to make cold calls about a product I didn't believe in.*

Producer—*I was expected to work more than forty hours per week regularly. I can do that as an exception but not the rule.*

11. Give an example of when you were able to contribute to a team project.

    Grower—*I was able to provide a different way of looking at the problem.*

    Chief—*I was able to suggest another team member who really helped us find a solution.*

    Implementor—*The team was in disarray until I provided a plan outlining how we should proceed.*

    Reckoner—*No one was considering the cost of their solutions. I provided an ROI analysis to show which potential solution was the best financially.*

    Peddler—*No one was interested in taking on the project until I joined the team. I was able to convince five people to join, and we got it done.*

    Producer—*I was able to talk about how management's ideas impacted the workers.*

I suggest you add the following questions to your standard interview questions:

12. What unique skills do you bring to a team? Give an example.

Grower—*I am good at seeing opportunities for expansion.*

Chief—*I am good at organizing people to address an issue.*

Implementor—*I am good at implementing the ideas leaders come up with.*

Reckoner—*I make sure we stay on task and avoid "mission creep."*

Peddler—*I am really good at communicating company direction to other employees in the right way.*

Producer—*I make sure the job gets done.*

13. What can you do day after day without tiring?

    Grower—*I can problem-solve and spin ideas all day long.*

    Chief—*I really enjoy helping people reach their potential.*

    Implementor—*I enjoy breaking down tasks and focusing those I supervise to accomplish them.*

    Reckoner—*Give me a situation or issue... I love to research all aspects of it.*

    Peddler—*I love talking to people about how customers love the company's services.*

    Producer—*Being outdoors, hiking, camping, surfing, you name it.*

14. Tell me about a time you felt you were in the wrong job or that someone else could do your job better than you.

    Grower—*My last employer assigned me to implement a new company initiative. I am better at idea generation than implementation.*

    Chief—*My job was to launch a new product line, but the government regulations confused me. Someone more detail-oriented would have been better.*

Implementor—*I was new and in a new role at my last job. My boss told me to create my own job description. I am much better at knowing exactly what is expected of me.*
Reckoner—*I was moved from my accountant role into management. I didn't like having to deal with the ambiguity of personnel issues.*
Peddler—*I was moved into an HR role because I had studied that a little in school. I could do it but hated it. I'm much better at talking with customers than employees.*
Producer—*My last job required me to work fifty-plus hours per week. I love working but am committed to a balanced work and homelife. That job was better suited for someone wanting to climb the corporate ladder, not me.*

In all the examples above, the job candidates gave you a clue to their innate ability. It can't be faked. Your challenge is to sit back and listen more intently for the hints. If you interview in teams, it is helpful for the other interviewers to employ this strategy as well and then compare notes after the interview. You don't have to change your existing interview questions—except to add the last three in my example.

I also suggest you have a candidate answer the following: *(You'll have to give them a pencil and paper for this one).*

> Order from most like you to least like you. (1 = most like you. 6 = least like you. Use all six numbers by placing one by each statement; use all the numbers, and do not use a number more than once.) On the job, my focus is best:
> ___On coming up with novel solutions.

____On the people who need to be mobilized to accomplish a goal.
____On lining out the tasks that need to be completed.
____On making sure the company is accountable.
____On broadcasting the successful outcomes to others.
____On keeping your head down and doing the work that's needed.

In evaluating their responses, these statements are listed in order: grower, chief, implementor, reckoner, peddler, producer.

The easiest position to match innate ability with job description and résumé is an accountant. Generally, companies want reckoners in accounting positions, and normally that will be the ability most applicants will have baked in. Just the fact that candidates graduated in accounting increases the probability they are reckoners.[3] Now, if they meet whatever résumé requirements you have, you found the right person for the job.

But what if you want to hire a lead to supervise a team of accountants? The innate ability for that role would likely be an implementor. So, now it gets a little more complicated. You want an implementer who happens to also have an accounting background. This is a bird of a different feather and necessitates figuring out if a candidate has the implementor innate ability, which you can easily screen for.

What if you want to hire a CFO to head a whole accounting department and proactively provide information to upper management? The field of candidates narrows even further. You will need to hire someone with the chief innate ability. This is a rarer person but one you need to find for them and the company to be successful. They exist, and you will find one by screening for that innate ability in someone with an accounting background.

I am sometimes asked which innate ability a CEO or equivalent should have. My answer is dependent on the stage of the company. In the start-up stages, growers make the best CEOs because the landscape is shifting, and creativity is needed at the top leadership positions. In a mature company, a chief is best because of their ability to lead and organize people. I have seen implementors and reckoners in the CEO role, but they tend to micromanage. Surprisingly, the success of the CEO is dependent on their right-hand person. If the CEO is a grower, their number one should be a chief or implementor. If a chief, their go-to should be an implementor. If an implementor or reckoner, their secondary would ideally be a grower or chief; however, this combination is the most difficult because the implementor or reckoner boss will have a tendency to squelch a grower and be threatened by a chief.

I met Sara a short time ago. She was recently hired as the new CEO of a large education and therapy organization. The previous CEO resigned because of board overreach, causing a significant upheaval and bad blood between the board and CEO. I was brought in initially to train the board on the importance of staying in their lane. I was later asked to facilitate the organization's annual strategic planning meeting.

To my surprise, my liaison with the company for the planning meeting was not Sara but with Tonia, the COO. Tonia was the one who organized the strategic planning meeting and the one people were to report to as they worked on their portion of the plan throughout the year. I couldn't figure out why until I realized Sara was a reckoner and Tonia a chief. Sara's background was with an accrediting organization where she did audits. Tonia's previous experience was in a leadership role with the US Military. Sara was more comfortable looking at financial and program outcome data than leading a team, whereas directing people was Tonia's bailiwick. Sara was not threatened by Tonia, and Tonia had no desire to be the CEO. They each appreciated the skills the other brought to the table. Theirs is an excellent, successful example of a reckoner CEO assisted by a chief COO.

CHAPTER 14

Right People, Right Time

> "The tragedy of life doesn't lie in not reaching
> your goal. The tragedy lies in having
> no goals to reach."
> —Benjamin Mays

Several years ago, one of my office buildings burned to the ground. Thankfully, no one was hurt, but I remember thinking, *What are we going to do now?* Businesses sometimes face challenges they can't control, like an economic downturn, bank collapse, pandemic, or natural disaster. During these times, the innate abilities of key personnel can be mobilized strategically. In my company's case, the local leader, a chief, took over, organized everyone, and moved the workforce to another location. Life carried on.

All businesses need to pay attention to the *right now*, the *near future*, and the *far future*. In short, the *right now* is attending to what you get paid to do. The *near future* are plans that move the company forward in a positive direction beyond the status quo within the year. They aren't too much of a stretch—things like a strategic goal not started yet, an almost-ready product launch, or a strategic hire. *Far future* ideas are at least a year out, maybe several, in the future. Among these could be the company's BHAGs (big hairy audacious goals), as Jim Collins and Jerry

Porras call them in their business classic *Build to Last*.[1] They are significant stretches for the company. Maybe it's a merger, expanding internationally, or simply creating a more interactive website that can't be afforded now.

If a company is totally focused on the *right now*, it's like the proverbial sticking your head in the sand, where people don't look up to see what's going on. A company in this position will fail eventually because they are not adapting to a changing market. Think BlackBerry or Nokia. These companies are still around but are largely irrelevant in the industry. What works or is popular now likely won't be in the future unless your product is Coca-Cola. But even the Coca-Cola Company isn't focused on the right now; look back at how their advertising and product line has changed over the years.

A company will struggle if it is too *near* or *far* focused because they aren't taking care of what brings in the money. They are guilty of having their proverbial head in the clouds. Think Takata airbags or Hasbro's Easy-Bake Oven. They ignored current product safety. While the companies survived the recalls, the debacles set them back. If you are big like Google, Apple, or Microsoft, you can experiment with Google Glass, the Newton, or Zune, but make sure your current offerings—the company's bread and butter—are solid.

There isn't an ideal ratio of how much time, money, and energy a company should devote to each category; it depends. One year, a company might spend 95 percent on *right now*, 4 percent on *near future*, and 1 percent on *far future* goals. That was certainly the case for my company during the COVID-19 pandemic. Like many companies, our focus was one-hundred-percent on the right now for a few months. That worked very well as a short-term solution to survive the emergency, but it is not a long-term answer. For some companies, the ratio one year might be 60, 35, and 5, or 40, 20, or 40 percent—or something else another year. For example, a few years ago, I challenged the board of a nonprofit organization I was consulting with to shift its focus away from the here and now and adopt a 5 percent, 60 percent, and 35 percent strategy. They needed desperately to expand their offerings or remain stagnant. Their *right now* was perfect and would take care of itself for a while, but they had nothing in the tank to move them beyond the status quo. The results were that multiple new income-producing initiatives were created, their offerings expanded, and funding increased. The point is that efforts were being made to consider all three areas in strategic planning.

I have facilitated hundreds of planning sessions for small start-ups and long-established national organizations over the years. As part of my facilitation, I have participants do prework by answering the following question: "What three things need to happen this year for you to be satisfied with the company's progress?" They email their answers to me, and I consolidate and categorize them. I do this so we can start running when we meet face-to-face or virtually as a group. Based on the answers I receive, I can peg who represents which innate abilities in the company. Some people write about operational improvement, *right now* things. Others are interested in BHAG objectives, *far future*, and some in-between, *near future* suggestions. Figure 2 illustrates where people and their innate abilities tend to focus their suggestions.

Figure 2

RIGHT NOW	NEAR FUTURE	FAR FUTURE

GROWERS

CHIEFS

IMPLEMENTORS

RECKONERS

PEDDLERS

PRODUCERS

I experienced two groups with homogeneous innate abilities when I started facilitating strategic plans. The first was a group of accountants assigned by their CEO to devise a plan for their department. They were the only people attending, and all were reckoners. They could only focus on the right now, and I failed to move them to consider near or far future objectives. On another occasion, I facilitated for a national organization's board; they were all growers. It was a fun meeting to facilitate, with a lot of energy and ideas flung about, but they had difficulty considering anything other than far future objectives. Both groups felt the meeting was productive and their plan outstanding. The reality was neither the reckoners' nor the growers' plans were worth the paper they were written on, and I'm sure they ended up in a drawer somewhere. The accountants restated what they were currently doing in their plan, and the board members didn't consider the realities of implementing their BHAGs. I now provide guidance on who should be present. It is important to have creative people with various innate abilities at the meeting.

Strategic plans that reflect right now, near, and far future objectives are all great for allocating corporate resources and time, but what happens when a crisis occurs? What innate ability is best to take charge when existing plans must be thrown out the window and new strategies implemented immediately? See figure 3.

At the start of this chapter, I mentioned that when my office building burned down, the local leader, who happened to have the chief innate ability, took over. She got everyone and everything lined out and moved forward within a few days. As a grower, I was still musing over how to buy a new building when she had another one leased and people back to work. I would have been too slow. Implementors and producers would still await their marching orders, and the reckoners and peddlers would pause for the dust to settle.

Figure 3

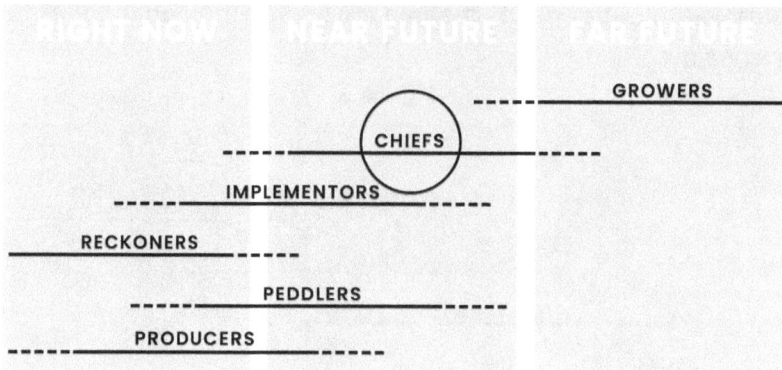

In old Western movies, when the wagon train was attacked, the trail boss would circle the wagons for protection. In a business sense, circling the wagons is focusing all energies on continuing to bring in the money and ensuring the company isn't bleeding financially. This is where the implementors, reckoners, and producers come in. That is what they do best. See figure 4.

Figure 4

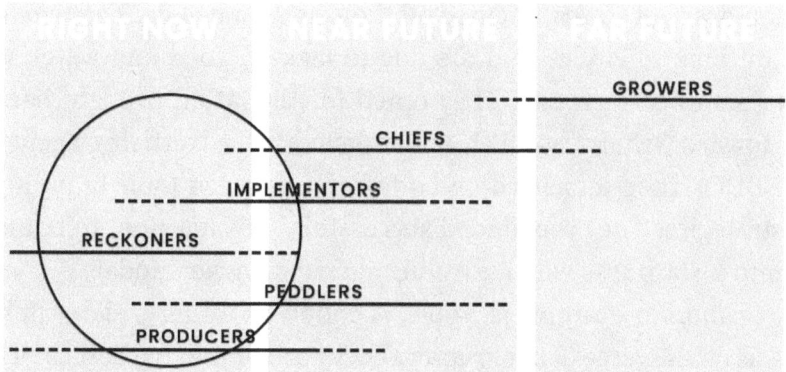

The Western settlers couldn't stay encircled for long; they would run out of food and water. Eventually, someone had to break free and go for help. Similarly, a company cannot hunker down indefinitely, or it will figuratively die from lack of food and water—growth. This is when to employ the growers and let them spin. See figure 5. Who knows? The company's long-term survival might depend on some crazy idea implemented at the right time.

Figure 5

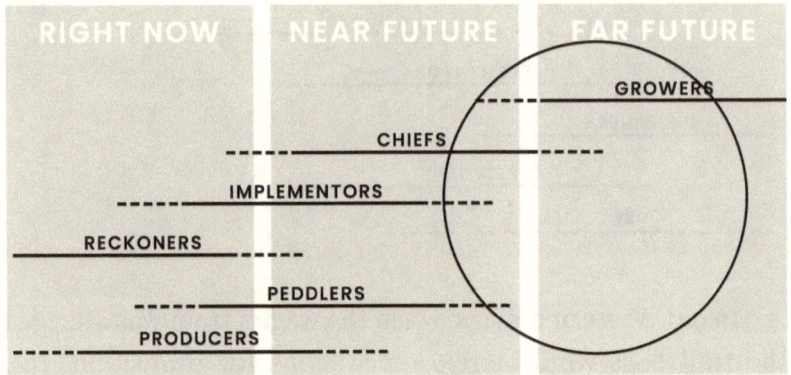

A good example is Starbucks. It had established itself as a global brand and expanded its offerings to include the music industry. In 2008, it had its crisis, partly due to the economic collapse. Its stock was falling. They circled their wagons, closed hundreds of stores, and laid off thousands of people. They could continue to circle—and die due to lack of "food and water"— or send for a grower. They opted for the latter, brought back Howard Schultz as CEO, and enlisted the advertising agency BBDO. They refocused on coffee and changed their branding strategies. They rebounded successfully. It's hard not to bump into a Starbucks when traveling almost anywhere today.

Another example is Apple. A couple of decades ago, Apple was on the verge of bankruptcy. They had some of the best chiefs, implementors, and reckoners circling the wagons and failing to stem the tide. They were losing billions. I remember that time and thinking, *Maybe I should buy some Apple stock*. I didn't because I believed the industry experts who predicted their demise. I didn't want to have a handful of worthless stock. Apple reached out to a grower, Steve Jobs, in 1997. The board had forced Jobs out of the company a decade before, ironically setting the stage for their company crisis that brought him back. With Jobs in the saddle, the company made one of the most remarkable turnarounds in history. Apple products are ubiquitous now, and it is one of the most valuable companies in the world. If I had bought the stock when tempted, I would be holding a pile of money.

The consequences of not having the right people with the right innate ability in the right positions at the right time can be catastrophic. Kris was the CEO of a small international child advocacy organization. He asked me to consult with his organization a few years ago. They were floundering, and I identified that part of the problem was that the organization lacked leadership with the chief ability. Kris is a peddler, and everyone loves him. He is deeply passionate about kids, and it will rub off on you after a few minutes of talking with him. He can light up a room and is the best fundraiser I have ever met. But when the COVID-19 restrictions hit, the organization was not prepared. The restrictions killed much of the organization's fee-for-service income. The organization lacked the chief ability on staff to respond. Rather than responding to the crisis by working on domestic opportunities, which a chief would have likely done, Kris, the peddler, took out loans and spent company resources to travel abroad to promote the organization. Kris lacked the skills to fix the holes in his organization's bucket and was unwilling to hire someone who did. His go-to solution was to ignore the *right now* opportunities and shoot for the moon. Kris's strategy might have worked with time, but the organization couldn't keep the doors open to see. They ran out of money because they had no *right now* business to generate it.

People with various innate abilities can be used at different stages in a company. Not only can and should they be used to best strategize *right now, near future,* and *far future* objectives for a company's current operations, but they should be used strategically during times of crisis. There is a time to hunker down and circle the wagons, and there is a time to break free and run for help. There are corresponding innate abilities to be employed for each phase.

CHAPTER 15

Four Quadrants

*"Technology does not run an enterprise.
Relationships do."*
—Patricia Fripp

Table 4

	Good Quality	Bad Quality
Good Relationship	1st Quadrant **Bright future.**	2nd Quadrant **Time to fix it.**
Bad Relationship	3rd Quadrant **Gotcha.**	4th Quadrant **No future.**

I distinctly remember the meeting when the concept of the four quadrants popped into my head. I met with the leaders of my nonprofit organization in the early 2000s. Over the years, we had grown the organization, expanding the service array into multiple states. We employed a little over a thousand people at the time. Some leaders were thriving, continuing to grow their divisions despite having some program quality issues. Others were losing business despite excellent service quality reviews. I was puzzled by this dilemma; all these people had big hearts, were trained and competent, and had good experiences before being put in leadership positions. Why the difference? Then, it hit me: those floundering focused on the wrong thing; ironically, they did so because of their innate ability. The chiefs and peddlers had great relationships with stakeholders but didn't pay as much attention to quality. The implementors and reckoners had virtually no relationship with the stakeholders, but service quality was spot on.

I quickly sketched out the four quadrants shown in table 4. I drew four squares and wrote "good quality" and "bad quality" along the top and "good relationship" and "bad relationship" along the side. Based on my experience, I then filled in the intersections.

Defining who you should foster a relationship with is essential when implementing the four quadrants. Broadly defined, you should foster a relationship with anyone you personally interact with who affects your business (customers, clients, funders, government regulators, employees, volunteers, consumers, etc.). Establishing a good relationship with a stakeholder you never see will have different challenges than those you interact with face-to-face. A customer who buys services from you, a government regulator who reviews what you do, and the employees who work for you will require different and purposeful planning to cultivate their relationship. The bottom line is having a relationship where they like you, your company, your product, and your service. If the relationship is one-on-one, are they your friend? Do you look forward to interactions with them? Can you see their face light up when they see you? You don't have to be bridge or golfing buddies or even friends on Facebook, but you need mutual trust and respect.

In understanding the four quadrants, defining what quality means for your business is important. Volumes have been written about quality and how to attain and maintain it. It is industry-dependent; making widgets requires different standards than providing home health care. At its elemental level, quality is best defined by the stakeholders.[1] Does your product or service meet or exceed stakeholders' expectations? In short, you don't determine what quality is; your stakeholders do. They expect products to be manufactured without flaws and services delivered with a smile.

With the established definitions of relationship and quality, I will explain each of the four quadrants, their implications for your business, and how people with various innate abilities can be strategically used.

Good relationship and good quality—at this intersection, your business has a bright future. It doesn't get better than this combination. Your great relationship with your stakeholders is enhanced by the quality of your product or service. In this situation, leaders with any of the innate abilities will thrive.

Good relationship and bad quality—in this combination, the stakeholders will give you time to fix the quality. If you do, life goes on its merry way. If you don't, it may ruin your relationship, and your one-time friend may become an enemy. As Rick Riordan stated, "No one can hate you more than someone who used to love you."[2] That is why divorces often turn nasty and why disaffected employees, church congregants, and club members sometimes turn on the organizations they once treasured. Your stakeholders are no different.

In my organization, the leaders with bad quality were chiefs with peddlers under them. They had great relationships with state funders but lacked the attention to detail to address the quality deficits in their operations. We didn't have to change the leaders to fix the issues; instead, people were deployed with the implementor's innate ability to assist. They fixed the quality issues, and within six months, we could move their operations from the second to first quadrant.

Bad relationship and good quality—my leaders who fell into the third quadrant were implementors assisted by producers. They were so focused on providing exemplary services that they neglected to build positive personal relationships with stakeholders (in our case, government funders). They thought all they had to do was deliver great services, and the rest would take care of itself. And while good services were necessary, neglecting to foster stakeholder relationships was an impediment. Some of the state funders felt negatively toward the leaders, but rather than trying to work on the relationship, the leaders doubled down on quality. This effort didn't move the relationship needle at all; instead, it set up a situation where any lapse of quality, real or imagined by the funder, resulted in a "gotcha" scenario. It was like the stakeholders were waiting for us to screw up and prove that their bad opinion of us was true.

We didn't have to fire current leaders to fix our quadrant three challenge; however, they needed help from people with the chief or peddler's ability to interface with the stakeholders because they are the best at building relationships. They became the contact people, not the implementors. It took about a year to improve the relationships to the point where the operations could move from the third to first quadrant.

Bad relationship and bad quality—this quadrant is corporate death. It isn't easy to come back from this situation. In our case, when an analysis revealed our service quality was terrible and we had no positive relationships among stakeholders, we threw in the towel in some instances and discontinued the operation. In other cases, we replaced the leadership and started over. We were eventually successful, but it took over a year, a lot of money, and leaders assisted by people with complementary innate abilities. We employed the crisis management approach described in chapter 14.

When I train management groups on the four quadrants, I ask, "Which is more important, quality or relationships?" The implementors, reckoners, and producers in the room say *quality*, and the growers, chiefs, and peddlers say *relationships*. The correct answer is relationships. Why? Because with a good relationship, if the quality deteriorates, you will likely be granted time to fix it. The better the relationship, the more time you have, but you do have to fix it.

This chapter aimed to illustrate how people with the various innate abilities might view problems and how they will default to try and fix them. Don't expect implementor and reckoner leaders to naturally consider the importance of fostering good relationships. I have attempted to train them to do so and failed. And when they do try, they stink at it. By the same token, don't expect growers, chiefs, and peddlers to instinctively prioritize quality; it's not their bailiwick.

CHAPTER 16

When it Works

> "The best time to plant a tree was twenty years ago. The second best time is now."
> —Chinese proverb

What is your best team experience? Have you ever worked with a group where everyone just clicked and accomplished whatever you were working on in short order? What was it about the team members? I wager it was more than them being okey-dokey people. In addition to their collegiality, I bet you experienced the synergy of the different innate abilities and didn't know it. There is nothing quite the same as a well-functioning team.

I taught leadership dynamics to doctoral management students for over fourteen years, and I have presented on innate abilities many times at national business leader conferences. My sessions are always well attended, not because I'm such a compelling presenter but because everyone struggles with surrounding themselves with the right team members. As part of the presentation, I have attendees identify who on their team is a grower, chief, implementor, reckoner, peddler, and producer. I give them the simple mountain climbing analogy I introduced in chapter 4. They write the first person on their team who comes to mind. I have also done this same exercise in one-on-one sessions with company heads. Most find the activity amusing, and everyone smiles at how easily they classify themselves and their team members. They can also identify gaps and if they have too many of a particular ability.

I then ask a question that catches them off guard. "If you were to reorganize your team and create team 2.0, who would stay and who would go?" I am always intrigued by how everyone in the room, sometimes several hundred people, has a simultaneous ah-ha moment. It's like the person leaps into their mind, and they want to shout their name. I generally randomly point at people in the audience and ask, "Did you think of someone?" "How about you?" "And you?" They always nod in agreement.

Identifying the type of people who should be on your team 2.0 is the easy part. Creating it from existing team members is the hard part. How easy is it to fire someone who is terrible at their job? How about mediocre? What about fair, good, or even excellent? As every personnel attorney will tell you, it is much easier to fire someone who is incompetent than outstanding. Although challenging, assembling a team based on innate abilities rather than their history will net better results. If everyone has the same innate abilities, you will not be as successful as you could be with diversity.

This book is not about how to fire team members—instead, how to assemble the most successful team you can. Hiring and promoting based on innate abilities works. I have seen it many times in organizations I have consulted with and have experienced it myself in my own companies. The following examples illustrate the benefit of team 2.0 decisions based on innate abilities.

I mentioned Ted in chapter 2. Ted was experienced and qualified for the VP of HR position. He did a great job with the mechanics of the job. Julie had no reason to terminate Ted based on his job performance. He was an excellent employee. The HR team members were implementors and reckoners. Unfortunately, Ted was also an implementor, and the department needed more leadership; it required a chief. Julie terminated Ted and hired a stranger, Morgan, who had experience and education in HR, but more importantly, Morgan was a chief. She has now been in that position for a decade, and the HR department has never been better.

I have consulted with a small nonprofit organization for six years, starting the year of its founding. They currently have two paid positions and use volunteers as needed. Mya, the CEO, depends on her board to fill the leadership gaps in the organization, which is typical of small nonprofits. A couple of years ago, Mya felt they weren't making any progress. She was frustrated. We examined the board members' abilities. Of the five members, she had one grower, one chief, two reckoners, and a producer. One issue with that configuration is that Mya is also a grower. The organization ended up spending too much time on *far future* objectives. Also, Mya and the grower board member clashed on their vision for the company. I recommended that the organization create Board 2.0, which was accomplished two months later. Some board members were retained, and others were asked to leave. Mya ended up with a working board comprised of a chief, an implementor, a reckoner, and a peddler. The difference is like night and day; the organization now has clear monetization objectives and is partnering with international agencies to broaden its reach.

The most dramatic transformation I've witnessed occurred in a company that quickly grew steadily during its first fifteen years, then plateaued. One of the owners and CEO retired. He was a chief. He hired his replacement. Unfortunately, he hired Jeff, an implementor. Implementors can make good CEOs if they have a chief as a COO or equivalent role under them; Jeff did not. He promoted one of the accounting staff, Kyle, who happened to be a reckoner. After two years, it became clear this needed to be fixed. The combination of implementor and reckoner made leadership prone to micromanage. They kept it together and improved procedures, but revenues decreased because they were bleeding clients. Jeff and Kyle created their own crisis by focusing on the trees and not the forest, and as business declined, they doubled down. They circled the corporate wagons and managed the organization to near death by only focusing on the *right now*. I was brought in by the owners to take over management. I terminated Jeff, and Kyle resigned that same day. I hired Levi as the new CEO. He was new to the role, something he could be mentored on, and he brought his grower ability with him, something he couldn't be trained on. He promoted Zoe from within, a chief, as the COO and, with her knowledge of operations, retained or replaced implementors who headed various departments. Levi reengaged the peddlers whom Jeff had sidelined and assigned to administrative tasks. He even brought in a private equity partner to fund much-needed expansion money. With a leadership team with the right innate abilities, Levi steered the company forward, increasing the company's value by 1,667 percent in four years. The owners sold their interest to the private equity partner and exited all smiles.

CHAPTER 17

Conclusion

"Success is often achieved by those who don't know that failure is inevitable."
—Coco Chanel

You can continue to hire the same way you have always done, but you will continue to get the same results. Innate ability hiring adds a third factor to your hiring protocol that significantly increases the odds of you hiring the right person for the job. It's not just a matter of education and experience that qualifies someone for a job or how well their interview went. Those are important, but equally essential is determining a candidate's innate ability. Does it match the expectations for the role? If you need to hire a chief and all applicants are something else, unless you are totally desperate, don't hire them. Do you need an implementor or a reckoner? Then make sure the one you choose has that innate ability.

Now that you know what to listen for, you can practice identifying innate ability in those around you. The more you do, the better you will get until you find yourself with just a few cues, being able to say, "He's a grower" or "She's a chief." By way of review, consider the simple mountain climbing analogy presented in chapter 4 to help your identification:

- Grower—the person who mortgages their home to buy a mountain.
- Chief—the person who organizes a team to climb the mountain.
- Implementor—the person who ensures everyone packs a lunch on the hike.
- Reckoner—the person who brings a map to ensure the group follows the right trail.
- Peddler—the person who sells the movie rights to the experience.
- Producers—the people who carry everyone else's water.

Or, if it is more helpful, contemplate the football analogy also mentioned in chapter 4:

- Grower—the team owner.
- Chief—the coach.
- Implementor—the quarterback.
- Reckoner—the people keeping statistics.
- Peddler—the people selling advertising and sponsorships.
- Producers—the players.

How you currently hire and promote isn't working. It's time to change. Add innate abilities to your hiring process and match the ability with the need in addition to whatever practices you currently use. You will be glad you did. Who knows? Maybe you will also experience a 1,667 percent return on your investment.

Chapter Notes

Introduction
1. Lou Adler, "Hiring is a Game of Chance—Here Are Your Odds," *LinkedIn* (August 20, 2018). https://www.linkedin.com/pulse/hiring-game-probability-here-your-odds-lou-adler

Chapter 1
1. Jeff McCoy, "Eight Percent of Americans Have Embellished Their Resume, Says New FindLaw.Com Survey," *Legal Current* (May 23, 2012). https://www.legalcurrent.com/eight-percent-of-americans-have-embellished-their-resume-says-new-findlaw-com-survey/.
2. *Mark* Tutton, "Uncovering the Multi-Million Dollar Fake Degree Industry," *CNN* (January 12, 2010). https://www.cnn.com/2010/BUSINESS/01/11/fake.college.degrees/index.html#:~:text=George%20Gollin%2C%20a%20board%20member,degree%20will%20typically%20cost%20%241%2C000.
3. Zachary M. Seward, "MIT Admissions Dean Resigns after Fake Degrees Come to Light," *The Harvard Crimson* (April 26, 2007). https://www.thecrimson.com/article/2007/4/26/mit-admissions-dean-resigns-after-fake/.
4. For example:
    a. Indeed, "Interview Questions and Answers," (accessed November 7, 2023). https://www.indeed.com/hire/interview-questions.
    b. Aimee, "What Are Ten Common Interview Questions and How to Ace Them," *Facty* (April 21, 2020). https://facty.com/network/answers/things/what-are-ten-common-interview-questions-and-how-to-ace-them/.
    c. Vicky Oliver, "10 Common Job Interview Questions and How to Answer Them." *Harvard Business Review* (July 27, 2023). https://hbr.org/2021/11/10-common-job-interview-questions-and-how-to-answer-them.

d. The Muse. "Your Ultimate Guide to Answering the Most Common Interview Questions." *The Muse (December 19, 2019). https://www.themuse.com/advice/interview-questions-and-answers.*

5. See:
   a. Taylor Cotterell, "Council Post: A Little Biased? Interview Order Does Matter." *Forbes* (September 12, 2023). https://www.forbes.com/sites/forbeshumanresourcescouncil/2019/03/22/a-little-biased-interview-order-does-matter/?sh=bc9b5667f98e.
   b. Dirk D. Steiner and Jeffrey S. Rain. "Immediate and Delayed Primacy and Recency Effects in Performance Evaluation." *Journal of Applied Psychology* 74, no. 1 (1989): 136–42. https://doi.org/10.1037//0021-9010.74.1.136.
   c. Bennet B. Murdock, "The Serial Position Effect of Free Recall," *Journal of Experimental Psychology* 64, no. 5 (1962): 482–88. https://doi.org/10.1037/h0045106.
6. Helen De Cruz, "Three Reasons Why We Should Not Request Letters of Recommendation for Job Applications." Blog of the APA (blog) (May 10, 2021). https://blog.apaonline.org/2019/10/15/three-reasons-why-we-should-not-request-letters-of-recommendation-for-job-applications/.

Chapter 2

1. Laurence F. Peter and Raymond Hull. *The Peter Principle*. (New York: William Morrow, 1969).
2. Lou Adler, "Hiring is Game of Chance—Here Are Your Odds," *LinkedIn (August 20, 2018). https://www.linkedin.com/pulse/hiring-game-probability-here-your-odds-lou-adler*

Chapter 3

1. See:
   a. Kentucky Counseling Center, "Know the 5 Major Personality Traits and the Corresponding Career Choices," (September 21, 2023). https://kentuckycounselingcenter.com/know-the-5-factor-personality-traits-and-career-choices/.
   b. Maynard Brusman, "Leadership Personality: Do You Have the Right Big Five Traits?," *Working Resources* (accessed June 19, 2023). https://www.workingresources.com/professionaleffectivenessarticles/leadership-personality-do-you-have-the-right-big-five-traits.html.

2. Paul T. Costa, Paul T. and Robert R. McCrae. "The Revised Neo Personality Inventory (NEO-PI-R)." *The SAGE Handbook of Personality Theory and Assessment: Volume 2 — Personality Measurement and Testing*, 2008, 179–98. https://doi.org/10.4135/9781849200479.n9.
3. Testgorilla "Talent Assessment and Remote Hiring Guides." TestGorilla (blog) (accessed August 17, 2023). https://www.testgorilla.com/blog/big-five-ocean-test/.
4. See:
    a. Michigan State University, "The Big 5 Personality Traits in the Workplace: MSU Online" (accessed July 12, 2023). https://www.michiganstateuniversityonline.com/resources/leadership/lead-your-team-with-big-five-model/.
    b. The Myers-Briggs Company. "The History of the MBTI® Assessment," (accessed July 12, 2023). https://eu.themyersbriggs.com/en/tools/MBTI/Myers-Briggs-history.
5. Myers & Briggs Foundation. "The 16 MBTI® Personality Types," (accessed July 20, 2023). https://www.myersbriggs.org/my-mbti-personality-type/mbti-basics/the-16-mbti-types.htm.
6. University of Pennsylvania, "Personality Puzzler: Is There Any Science behind Myers-Briggs?" *Knowledge at Wharton* (November 8, 2018). https://knowledge.wharton.upenn.edu/podcast/knowledge-at-wharton-podcast/does-the-myers-briggs-test-really-work/.
7. Emma Goldberg, "Personality Tests Are the Astrology of the Office." *The New York Times* (September 17, 2019). https://www.nytimes.com/2019/09/17/style/personality-tests-office.html.
8. ZodiacSign.com. "Zodiac Signs and Astrology Signs Meanings and Characteristics." (accessed August 10, 2023). https://www.zodiacsign.com/.
9. See:
    a. ColorCode Personality Science. "Which Hue are You?" (accessed November 11, 2023). https://www.colorcode.com/.
    b. Drew D'Agostino, "Big Five vs. 16-Personalities." *Crystal Knows*, (accessed November 11, 2023). https://www.crystalknows.com/resource/big-five-vs-16-personality#:~:text=Strengths%3A%20The%20Big%20Five%20model,measurements%20for%20its%20individual%20traits.

    c. Jackson G. Lu, Xin Lucy Liu, Hui Liao, and Lei Wang. "Disentangling Stereotypes from Social Reality: Astrological Stereotypes and Discrimination in China," *Journal of Personality and Social Psychology* 119, no. 6 (2020): 1359–79. https://doi.org/10.1037/pspi0000237.

    d. 365 Tests, "Color Personality Test: What's Your True Personality Color?" (accessed January 12, 2024). https://365tests.com/personality-tests/free-color-personality-test/.

10. Goldberg, "Personality Tests are the Astrology of the Office."
11. Bernard Lown, *The Lost Art of Healing: Practicing Compassion in Medicine*. New York, NY: Ballantine Books, 1999.

Chapter 4

1. This is similar to a technique recommended by Catherine Nomura and Julia Waller, *Unique ability: Creating the Life You Want*. (Toronto, Canada: The Strategic Coach Inc), 25-29.

Chapter 5

1. See:

    a. Marcela Rodica Luca and A Robu, "Personality Traits in Entrepreneurs and Self-Employed" *Bulletin of the Transilvania University of Brasov Series III Mathematics and Computer Science* 9, no 58-2 (January 2016): 91-98. https://www.researchgate.net/publication/312320488_PERSONALITY_TRAITS_IN_ENTREPRENEURS_AND_SELF-EMPLOYED.

    b. Dale Archer, "ADHD: The Entrepreneur's Superpower," *Forbes (October 12, 2022)*. https://www.forbes.com/sites/dalearcher/2014/05/14/adhd-the-entrepreneurs-superpower/?sh=7ddf89ae59e9.

    c. Roy Thurik, Anis Khedhaouria, Olivier Torrès, and Ingrid Verheul, "ADHD Symptoms and Entrepreneurial Orientation of Small Firm Owners," *Applied Psychology* 65, no 3 (February 2016): 568-586. https://doi.org/10.1111/apps.12062

    d. Isabella Hatak, Manling Chang, Rainer Harms, and Johan Wiklund, "ADHD Symptoms, Entrepreneurial Passion, and Entrepreneurial Performance—Small Business Economics." *Small Business Economics 57, no 4 (2020):1693-1713*. https://link.springer.com/article/10.1007/s11187-020-00397-x.

2. Bonnie Farber Canziani and Dianne H.B. Welsh. "How Entrepreneurship Influences Other Disciplines: An Examination of Learning Goals." *The International Journal of Management Education* 19, no 1 (March 2019): 100278. https://www.sciencedirect.com/science/article/abs/pii/S1472811718303112.

3. See:

    a. Alison Milligton, "J.K. Rowling's Pitch for 'Harry Potter' Was Rejected 12 Times—Read the Now-Famous Letter Here," *Business Insider* (July 31, 2018). https://www.insider.com/revealed-jk-rowlings-original-pitch-for-harry-potter-2017-10.

    b. Julie Tucker, "From Secretary to Billionaire Author… JK Rowling Life Before Harry," *Headspace* (blog) (accessed November 1, 2023). https://www.headspacegroup.co.uk/from-secretary-to-billionaire-author-jk-rowlings-life-before-harry/#:~:text=After%20graduating%20from%20university%2C%20Rowling,a%20career%20at%20that%20time.

4. See:

    a. Chaoyun Liang (2019). "How Entrepreneur Personality Affects Agrirural Entrepreneurial Alertness," *Journal of Entrepreneurship, Management and Innovation* 15, no 1 (2019): 147-169. https://doi.org/10.7341/20191516.

    b. Hermann Brandstätter, "Personality Aspects of Entrepreneurship: A Look at Five Meta-Analyses." *Personality and Individual Differences* 51, no. 3 (2011): 222–30. https://doi.org/10.1016/j.paid.2010.07.007.

    c. Irum Alvi and Manisha Vyas. "Entrepreneurial Intent and Personal Traits—Role of Entrepreneurship Education." *The Journal of Management Awareness* 23, no. 2 (2020): 1–13. https://doi.org/10.5958/0974-0945.2020.00006.0.

5. See:

    a. Diego Aboal and Federico Veneri, "Entrepreneurs in Latin America." *Small Business Economics* 46, no. 3 (2016): 503–25. https://doi.org/10.1007/s11187-015-9696-3.

    b. Hermann Brandstätter, "Personality Aspects of Entrepreneurship: A Look at Five Meta-Analyses."

    c. Wayne H. Stewart and Philip L. Roth. "Data Quality Affects Meta-Analytic Conclusions: A Response to Miner and Raju Concerning Entrepreneurial Risk Propensity," *Journal of Applied Psychology* 89, no. 1 (2004): 14–21. https://doi.org/10.1037/0021-9010.89.1.14.

6. See:
    a. Hermann Brandstätter, "Personality Aspects of Entrepreneurship: A Look at Five Meta-Analyses." *Personality and Individual Differences* 51, no. 3 (2011): 222–30. https://doi.org/10.1016/j.paid.2010.07.007.
    b. Farber Canziani, Bonnie, and Dianne H.B. Welsh. "How Entrepreneurship Influences Other Disciplines: An Examination of Learning Goals." *The International Journal of Management Education* 19, no. 1 (2021): 100278. https://doi.org/10.1016/j.ijme.2019.01.003.
    c. Yannick Dillen, Eddy Laveren, Rudy Martens, Sven De Vocht, and Eric Van Imschoot. "From 'Manager' to 'Strategist.'" *International Journal of Entrepreneurial Behavior and Research* 25, no. 1 (2019): 2–28. https://doi.org/10.1108/ijebr-01-2017-0010.

Chapter 6

1. See:
    a. Philippe Jacquart and John Antonakis, "When Does Charisma Matter for Top-Level Leaders? Effect of Attributional Ambiguity," *Academy of Management Journal* 58, no. 4 (2015): 1051–74. https://doi.org/10.5465/amj.2012.0831.
    b. Deana Raffo and Ralph Williams. "Evaluating Potential Transformational Leaders: Weighing Charisma vs. Credibility." *Strategy and Leadership* 46, no. 6 (2018): 28–34. https://doi.org/10.1108/sl-12-2017-0130.
2. Alan Anderson, *Management: Take Charge of Your Team* (5th ed). Self-published.
3. See:
    a. Inspiring Leadership Now, "10 of the Most Inspiring Leaders of All Time: Remarkable Stories of Iconic Trail Blazers Who Went from Adversity to Extraordinary & Redefined Leadership." *Inspiring Leadership Now* (blog) (April 2, 2020). https://www.inspiringleadershipnow.com/most-inspiring-leaders-redefine-leadership/.
    b. Gov.uk, "Sir Winston Churchill," *Gov.uk* (accessed August 11, 2023). https://www.gov.uk/government/history/past-prime-ministers/winston-churchill.
4. Seth Godin, *Tribes: We Need You to Lead Us* (New York, NY: Penguin, 2008).
5. See:

    a. William Arruda, "9 Differences Between Being a Leader and a Manager," *Forbes* (September 12, 2023). https://www.forbes.com/sites/williamarruda/2016/11/15/9-differences-between-being-a-leader-and-a-manager/#454e3c1b4609.

    b. Robert N. Lussier and Christopher F. Achua, *Leadership: Theory, application, and skill development* (Thousand Oaks, CA: Sage Publications Inc, 2023).

Chapter 7

1. Jim Clifton and James Harter, *It's the Manager: Moving from Boss to Coach* (New York, NY: Gallup Press, 2020).
2. Wikipedia, "Jen O'Malley Dillon" (accessed January 7, 2024). https://en.wikipedia.org/wiki/Jen_O%27Malley_Dillon.
3. See:

    a. Hermann Brandstätter, "Personality Aspects of Entrepreneurship: A Look at Five Meta-Analyses," *Personality and Individual Differences* 51, no. 3 (2011): 222–30. https://doi.org/10.1016/j.paid.2010.07.007.

    b. Arruda, William. "9 Differences between Being a Leader and a Manager." Forbes, September 12, 2023. https://www.forbes.com/sites/williamarruda/2016/11/15/9-differences-between-being-a-leader-and-a-manager/#454e3c1b4609.

Chapter 8

1. Wikipedia, "Time Person of the Year," (accessed November 11, 2023). https://en.wikipedia.org/wiki/Time_Person_of_the_Year.
2. Wikipedia, "Cynthia Cooper (Accountant)," (accessed November 11, 2023). https://en.wikipedia.org/wiki/Cynthia_Cooper_(accountant).
3. Wikipedia, "Sherron Watkins," (accessed November 11, 2023). https://en.wikipedia.org/wiki/Sherron_Watkins.
4. See:

    a. Susan P. Briggs,, Scott Travis Copeland, and David Haynes. "Accountants for the 21st Century, Where Are You? A Five-Year Study of Accounting Students' Personality Preferences." Critical Perspectives on Accounting" (July 2007): 511–37. https://doi.org/10.1016/j.cpa.2006.01.013.

    b. Larry Kresier, Joseph M. McKeon, and Alan Post, "A Personality Profile of CPAs in Public Practice," *The Ohio CPA Journal* (1990): 29–34.

  c. Stacy Kovar, Richard L. Ott, and Dann G. Fisher. "Personality Preferences of Accounting Students: A Longitudinal Case Study." *Journal of Accounting Education* 21, no. 2 (April 2003): 75–94. https://doi.org/10.1016/s0748-5751(03)00008-3.

  d. Stephen F. Laribee, "The Psychological Types of College Accounting Students," *Journal of Psychological Type* 28 (1994): 37-42. https://psycnet.apa.org/record/1994-45088-001

  e. Paul G. Schloemer and Melanie S Schloemer, "The Personality Types and Preferences of CPA Firm Professionals: An Analysis of Changes in the Profession," *American Accounting Association* 11 (December 1997): 24–39. https://www.proquest.com/docview/208912115?pq-origsite=gscholar&fromopenview=true&sourcetype=Scholarly%20Journals

5. See:

  a. Jacob J. Levy, John D. Richardson, John W. Lounsbury, Destin Stewart, Lucy W. Gibson, and Adam W. Drost, "Personality Traits and Career Satisfaction of Accounting Professionals," *Individual Differences Research* 9, no. 4 (2011): 238–49.

  b. Lisa McQuerrey, "Traits, Skills, and Personal Characteristics for an Accountant." *Chron* (March 23, 2018). https://work.chron.com/traits-skills-personal-characteristics-accountant-9716.html.

  c. Guy W. Trump and H.S. Hendrickson. "Education and Professional Training. Employer firm selection among accounting majors: An ex-post study," *The Journal of Accountancy* 131, no. 4 (1972): 87–89.

Chapter 9

1. See:

  a. Sandra Castro-González and Belén Bande, "The Changing Role of the Salesperson: How Should Salespeople Act Today?" *Development and Learning in Organizations: An International Journal* 33, no. 6 (2019): 8–11. https://doi.org/10.1108/dlo-11-2018-0142.

  b. Avner Caspi, Ronit Bogler, and Ofir Tzuman. "'Judging a Book by Its Cover': The Dominance of Delivery over Content When Perceiving Charisma." *Group & Organization Management* 44, no. 6 (2019): 1067–98. https://doi.org/10.1177/1059601119835982.

  c. Steve W. Martin, "Seven Personality Traits of Top Salespeople,"

Harvard Business Review (July 23, 2014). https://hbr.org/2011/06/the-seven-personality-traits-0.

    d. Garry J. Smith, "The Narcissistic Salesperson: A Framework of Their Relationship with Job Satisfaction, Organizational Commitment, and Customer Orientation." *Atlantic Marketing Journal* 6, no 2 (November 2017): 1–21. https://digitalcommons.kennesaw.edu/cgi/viewcontent.cgi?article=1227&context=amj

2. See:

    a. Diana May-Jennings, "Top 9 Most Influential Salespeople of All Time." *SalesRabbit* (June 23, 2023). https://salesrabbit.com/insights/top-9-most-influential-salespeople-of-all-time/.

    b. Mike Mishkin, "Erica Feidner: Piano MatchmakerTM." *iLovetheUpperWestSide.com* (May 10, 2021). https://ilovetheupperwestside.com/erica-feidner-piano-matchmaker/.

3. Thomas E. DeCarlo and Son K. Lam. "Identifying Effective Hunters and Farmers in the Salesforce: A Dispositional–Situational Framework." *Journal of the Academy of Marketing Science* 44, no. 4 (2015): 415–39. https://doi.org/10.1007/s11747-015-0425-x.

4. Hermann Brandstätter, "Personality Aspects of Entrepreneurship: A Look at Five Meta-Analyses." *Personality and Individual Differences* 51, no. 3 (2011): 222–30. https://doi.org/10.1016/j.paid.2010.07.007.

5. Just Serve is a national initiative where the volunteer needs of organizations are posted and volunteers search for opportunities to serve. See, https://www.justserve.org

Chapter 10

1. See:

    a. Juliana LaBianca, "These People Donated Millions after They Died-but No One Knew They Were Rich." *Reader's Digest* (February 7, 2023). https://www.rd.com/article/secret-millionaires-donations-after-died/.

    b. Prosperity Thinkers, "Secret Millionaires: Everyday People, Extraordinary Wealth." (September 7, 2023). https://prosperitythinkers.com/personal-finance/secret-millionaires/.

2. Rent A Husband, (accessed January 12, 2024). https://www.rentahusbandinc.com/.

Chapter 11

1. Kolbe Corp, "Kolbe ATM Index," (accessed July 10, 2023). https://www.kolbe.com/kolbe-a-index/.
2. See:
    a. Kimberly Lucas, "Develop both Entrepreneurs and Leadership for Business Success," *Goldstone Partners* (July 31, 2020). https://www.goldstonepartners.com/entrepreneurship-vs-leadership/.
    b. William Arruda, "9 Differences between Being a Leader and a Manager." *Forbes*, (September 12, 2023). https://www.forbes.com/sites/williamarruda/2016/11/15/9-differences-between-being-a-leader-and-a-manager/#454e3c1b4609.
    c. Robert N. Lussier and Christopher F. Achua. *Leadership: Theory, application, and skill development* (Thousand Oaks, CA: Sage Publications Inc, 2023).
    d. Avner Caspi, Ronit Bogler, and Ofir Tzuman. "'Judging a Book by Its Cover': The Dominance of Delivery over Content When Perceiving Charisma." *Group & Organization Management* 44, no. 6 (2019): 1067–98. https://doi.org/10.1177/1059601119835982.
    e. Hermann Brandstätter, "Personality Aspects of Entrepreneurship: A Look at Five Meta-Analyses." *Personality and Individual Differences* 51, no. 3 (2011): 222–30. https://doi.org/10.1016/j.paid.2010.07.007.
    f. William Arruda, "9 Differences between Being a Leader and a Manager." *Forbes* (September 12, 2023). https://www.forbes.com/sites/williamarruda/2016/11/15/9-differences-between-being-a-leader-and-a-manager/#454e3c1b4609.
    g. Ellie Nieves, "Leadership vs Management: How to Differentiate and Why It Matters." *Fairygodboss* (October 19, 2021). https://fairygodboss.com/career-topics/leadership-vs-management.
    h. Alan Anderson, *Management: Take charge of your team: Communication, Leadership, Coaching and Conflict Resolution* (5rd ed) (CreateSpace Independent Publishing Platform, 2015).
    i. Lisa McQuerrey, "Traits, Skills, and Personal Characteristics for an Accountant." *Work (February 5, 2019)*. https://work.chron.com/traits-skills-personal-characteristics-accountant-9716.html.
    j. Susan Briggs, Scott Travis Copeland, and David Haynes, "Accountants for the 21st Century, Where Are You? A Five-Year Study of Accounting

Students' Personality Preferences." *Critical Perspectives on Accounting* 18, no 5 (July 2007): 511–37. https://doi.org/10.1016/j.cpa.2006.01.013.

k. Larry Kresier, Joseph M. McKeon, and Alan Post, "A Personality Profile of CPAs in Public Practice," *The Ohio CPA Journal* (1990): 29–34.

l. Stephen F. Laribee, "The Psychological Types of College Accounting Students," *Journal of Psychological Type* 28 (1994): 37-42. https://psycnet.apa.org/record/1994-45088-001Schloemer, m.

m. Paul G. Schloemer and Melanie S Schloemer, "The Personality Types and Preferences of CPA Firm Professionals: An Analysis of Changes in the Profession," *American Accounting Association* 11 (December 1997): 24–39. https://www.proquest.com/docview/208912115?pq-origsite=gscholar&fromopenview=true&sourcetype=Scholarly%20Journals

n. Garry J. Smith, "The Narcissistic Salesperson: A Framework of Their Relationship with Job Satisfaction, Organizational Commitment, and Customer Orientation." *Atlantic Marketing Journal* 6, no 2 (November 2017): 1–21. https://digitalcommons.kennesaw.edu/cgi/viewcontent.cgi?article=1227&context=amj

o. Steve W. Martin, "Seven Personality Traits of Top Salespeople," *Harvard Business Review* (July 23, 2014). https://hbr.org/2011/06/the-seven-personality-traits-o.

p. Sandra Castro-González and Belén Bande, "The Changing Role of the Salesperson: How Should Salespeople Act Today?" *Development and Learning in Organizations: An International Journal* 33, no. 6 (2019): 8–11. https://doi.org/10.1108/dlo-11-2018-0142.

q. Marcela Rodica Luca and A Robu, "Personality Traits in Entrepreneurs and Self-Employed" *Bulletin of the Transilvania University of Brasov Series III Mathematics and Computer Science* 9, no 58-2 (January 2016): 91-98. https://www.researchgate.net/publication/312320488_PERSONALITY_TRAITS_IN_ENTREPRENEURS_AND_SELF-EMPLOYED.

r. Diego Aboal and Federico Veneri, "Entrepreneurs in Latin America." *Small Business Economics* 46, no. 3 (2016): 503–25. https://doi.org/10.1007/s11187-015-9696-3.

s. Hermann Brandstätter, "Personality Aspects of Entrepreneurship: A Look at Five Meta-Analyses," *Personality and Individual Differences* 51, no. 3 (2011): 222–30. https://doi.org/10.1016/j.

paid.2010.07.007.

t. Stacy E. Kovar, Richard L. Ott, and Dann G. Fisher. "Personality Preferences of Accounting Students: A Longitudinal Case Study," *Journal of Accounting Education* 21, no. 2 (2003): 75–94. https://doi.org/10.1016/s0748-5751(03)00008-3.

Chapter 12

1. Raymond B. Cattell, "Theory of Fluid and Crystallized Intelligence: A Critical Experiment." *Journal of Educational Psychology* 54, no. 1 (1963): 1–22. https://doi.org/10.1037/h0046743.
2. Howard Gardner, *Multiple Intelligences: New Horizons in Theory in Practice*, (New York: BasicBooks, 2006).
3. See:
    a. Wikipedia, "Isaac Newton," (accessed July 10, 2023). https://en.wikipedia.org/wiki/Isaac_Newton.
    b. The Royal Mint Museum, "Isaac Newton, Warden and Master of the Royal Mint 1696-1727," (accessed November 11, 2023). https://www.royalmintmuseum.org.uk/journal/people/isaac-newton/.
    c. Thomas Leveson, *Newton and the counterfeiter: The unknown detective career of the world's greatest scientist,* (Boston, MA: Mariner Books, 2010).
    d. Findlay G. Shirras and J. H. Craig. "Sir Isaac Newton and the Currency," *The Economic Journal* 55, no. 218/219 (1945): 217. https://doi.org/10.2307/2226082.

Chapter 13

1. See:
    a. Myers-Briggs—https://www.myersbriggs.org
    b. Big Five—https://www.parinc.com/Products/Pkey/276
    c. Kolbe—https://www.kolbe.com/kolbe-a-index/
    d. Color Code—https://www.colorcode.com
2. Taken from:
    a. Indeed, "Opening and Closing Interview Questions," (accessed August 3, 2023). https://www.indeed.com/hire/c/info/opening-and-closing-interview-questions.
    b. Career One Stop, "Common Interview Questions." (accessed August 3, 2023). https://www.careeronestop.org/JobSearch/Interview/

common-interview-questions.aspx.

3. Stacy Kovar, Richard L. Ott, and Dann G. Fisher, "Personality Preferences of Accounting Students: A Longitudinal Case Study," *Journal of Accounting Education* 21, no. 2 (April 1, 2003): 75–94. https://doi.org/10.1016/s0748-5751(03)00008-3.

Chapter 14

1. Jim Collins and Jerry Porras. *Built to Last: Successful Habits of Visionary Companies.* (Winter Springs, FL: Paw Prints, 2011).

Chapter 15

1. Sean Peek, "The Management Theory of Joseph Juran." business.com (June 28, 2023). https://www.business.com/articles/management-theory-of-joseph-juran/#.

2. Rick Riordan, "A Quote from the Blood of Olympus." Goodreads (October 7, 2014). https://www.goodreads.com/quotes/6826136-no-one-can-hate-you-more-than-someone-who-used.

APPENDIX A

The Hiring Template

On a piece of paper, have your applicants complete the following:

Self-Rating

Order from 1 to 6, most like you to least like you, with 1 being most like you and 6 being least like you. Use every number and only once. *(There is no right order. We just want to get to know you a little better.)*

On the job, your focus is best:

___on coming up with novel solutions.

___on the people who need to be mobilized to accomplish a goal.

___on lining out the tasks that are needed to be completed.

___on making sure the company is accountable.

___on broadcasting the successful outcomes to others.

___on doing the work that's needed.

Add questions 13 and 14 to whatever relevant, appropriate, and legal question you already have used in the past in interviews.

Note their answers and mark in the square the innate ability their answer most resembles. It's okay if a candidate gives an answer that sounds like a reckoner to one question and a chief on another.

- **Grower** *(Focused on novel ideas. High tolerance for risk and ambiguity. Energized by new prospects. Creative and seeing opportunities where others don't.)*
- **Chief** *(People focused on accomplishing the objective. Medium-high risk-tolerant. Create a vision for others. Good at coaching and mentoring. Change agents. Willing to try new things. Influence the process. Understand a team is more effective than individuals.)*
- **Implementor** *(Tasked focused to accomplish the objective. Medium-low risk tolerant. Need an established vision. Good at organizing. Are process-oriented. Control various aspects of projects. Think short-term.)*
- **Reckoner** *(Focused on rules and accountability. Low risk tolerance. Organized and orderly. Have a set of standards they want to be followed. Gets things done in the most efficient way possible. Has excellent attention to detail.)*
- **Peddler** *(Focused on promotion of ideas. Medium-high risk tolerant. Achievement orientation. Friendly and likable. Assertive. High emotional intelligence.)*
- **Producer** *(Focused on doing the work. Medium-low risk-tolerant. Creativity is limited to the job at hand. Concrete thinkers. Low tolerance for ambiguity. Do not aspire to leadership positions. Separate work and personal life.)*

Your interview questions might look something like the following:

(Your Company) Position Interview Sheet

Candidate: _____

Your Name: _____

Date: _____ Time: _____

Job position to be hired: _____

Ideal innate ability for this role: Grower, Chief, Implementor, Reckoner, Peddler, Producer

Questions for the applicant. *(Note their answers and mark the innate ability you think their answer represents.)*

1. Tell me something about yourself that isn't on your résumé.

_____
_____
_____
_____
_____
_____
_____

- ❏ **Grower** *(Focused on novel ideas. High tolerance for risk and ambiguity. Energized by new prospects. Creative and seeing opportunities where others don't.)*
- ❏ **Chief** *(People focused on accomplishing the objective. Medium-high risk-tolerant. Create a vision for others. Good at coaching and mentoring. Change agents. Willing to try new things. Influence the process. Understand a team is more effective than individuals.)*
- ❏ **Implementor** *(Tasked focused to accomplish the objective. Medium-low risk tolerant. Need an established vision. Good at organizing. Are process-oriented. Control various aspects of projects. Think short-term.)*
- ❏ **Reckoner** *(Focused on rules and accountability. Low risk tolerance. Organized and orderly. Have a set of standards they want to be followed. Gets things done in the most efficient way possible. Has excellent attention to detail.)*
- ❏ **Peddler** *(Focused on promotion of ideas. Medium-high risk tolerant. Achievement orientation. Friendly and likable. Assertive. High emotional intelligence.)*
- ❏ **Producer** *(Focused on doing the work. Medium-low risk-tolerant. Creativity is limited to the job at hand. Concrete thinkers. Low tolerance for ambiguity. Do not aspire to leadership positions. Separate work and personal life.)*

2. Where do you see yourself in five years?

_____
_____
_____
_____
_____
_____

- ❏ **Grower** *(Focused on novel ideas. High tolerance for risk and ambiguity. Energized by new prospects. Creative and seeing opportunities where others don't.)*
- ❏ **Chief** *(People focused on accomplishing the objective. Medium-high risk-tolerant. Create a vision for others. Good at coaching and mentoring. Change agents. Willing to try new things. Influence the process. Understand a team is more effective than individuals.)*
- ❏ **Implementor** *(Tasked focused to accomplish the objective. Medium-low risk tolerant. Need an established vision. Good at organizing. Are process-oriented. Control various aspects of projects. Think short-term.)*
- ❏ **Reckoner** *(Focused on rules and accountability. Low risk tolerance. Organized and orderly. Have a set of standards they want to be followed. Gets things done in the most efficient way possible. Has excellent attention to detail.)*
- ❏ **Peddler** *(Focused on promotion of ideas. Medium-high risk tolerant. Achievement orientation. Friendly and likable. Assertive. High emotional intelligence.)*
- ❏ **Producer** *(Focused on doing the work. Medium-low risk-tolerant. Creativity is limited to the job at hand. Concrete thinkers. Low tolerance for ambiguity. Do not aspire to leadership positions. Separate work and personal life.)*

3. How would other people describe you?

_____
_____
_____
_____
_____
_____

- ❏ **Grower** *(Focused on novel ideas. High tolerance for risk and ambiguity. Energized by new prospects. Creative and seeing opportunities where others don't.)*
- ❏ **Chief** *(People focused on accomplishing the objective. Medium-high risk-tolerant. Create a vision for others. Good at coaching and mentoring. Change agents. Willing to try new things. Influence the process. Understand a team is more effective than individuals.)*
- ❏ **Implementor** *(Tasked focused to accomplish the objective. Medium-low risk tolerant. Need an established vision. Good at organizing. Are process-oriented. Control various aspects of projects. Think short-term.)*
- ❏ **Reckoner** *(Focused on rules and accountability. Low risk tolerance. Organized and orderly. Have a set of standards they want to be followed. Gets things done in the most efficient way possible. Has excellent attention to detail.)*
- ❏ **Peddler** *(Focused on promotion of ideas. Medium-high risk tolerant. Achievement orientation. Friendly and likable. Assertive. High emotional intelligence.)*
- ❏ **Producer** *(Focused on doing the work. Medium-low risk-tolerant. Creativity is limited to the job at hand. Concrete thinkers. Low tolerance for ambiguity. Do not aspire to leadership positions. Separate work and personal life.)*

4. What motivates you?

_____
_____
_____
_____
_____
_____

- ❑ **Grower** *(Focused on novel ideas. High tolerance for risk and ambiguity. Energized by new prospects. Creative and seeing opportunities where others don't.)*
- ❑ **Chief** *(People focused on accomplishing the objective. Medium-high risk-tolerant. Create a vision for others. Good at coaching and mentoring. Change agents. Willing to try new things. Influence the process. Understand a team is more effective than individuals.)*
- ❑ **Implementor** *(Tasked focused to accomplish the objective. Medium-low risk tolerant. Need an established vision. Good at organizing. Are process-oriented. Control various aspects of projects. Think short-term.)*
- ❑ **Reckoner** *(Focused on rules and accountability. Low risk tolerance. Organized and orderly. Have a set of standards they want to be followed. Gets things done in the most efficient way possible. Has excellent attention to detail.)*
- ❑ **Peddler** *(Focused on promotion of ideas. Medium-high risk tolerant. Achievement orientation. Friendly and likable. Assertive. High emotional intelligence.)*
- ❑ **Producer** *(Focused on doing the work. Medium-low risk-tolerant. Creativity is limited to the job at hand. Concrete thinkers. Low tolerance for ambiguity. Do not aspire to leadership positions. Separate work and personal life.)*

5. What are you most passionate about?
_____
_____
_____
_____
_____
_____

- ❏ **Grower** *(Focused on novel ideas. High tolerance for risk and ambiguity. Energized by new prospects. Creative and seeing opportunities where others don't.)*
- ❏ **Chief** *(People focused on accomplishing the objective. Medium-high risk-tolerant. Create a vision for others. Good at coaching and mentoring. Change agents. Willing to try new things. Influence the process. Understand a team is more effective than individuals.)*
- ❏ **Implementor** *(Tasked focused to accomplish the objective. Medium-low risk tolerant. Need an established vision. Good at organizing. Are process-oriented. Control various aspects of projects. Think short-term.)*
- ❏ **Reckoner** *(Focused on rules and accountability. Low risk tolerance. Organized and orderly. Have a set of standards they want to be followed. Gets things done in the most efficient way possible. Has excellent attention to detail.)*
- ❏ **Peddler** *(Focused on promotion of ideas. Medium-high risk tolerant. Achievement orientation. Friendly and likable. Assertive. High emotional intelligence.)*
- ❏ **Producer** *(Focused on doing the work. Medium-low risk-tolerant. Creativity is limited to the job at hand. Concrete thinkers. Low tolerance for ambiguity. Do not aspire to leadership positions. Separate work and personal life.)*

6. What are your weaknesses?
___
___
___
___
___
___
___

- ❏ **Grower** *(Focused on novel ideas. High tolerance for risk and ambiguity. Energized by new prospects. Creative and seeing opportunities where others don't.)*
- ❏ **Chief** *(People focused on accomplishing the objective. Medium-high risk-tolerant. Create a vision for others. Good at coaching and mentoring. Change agents. Willing to try new things. Influence the process. Understand a team is more effective than individuals.)*
- ❏ **Implementor** *(Tasked focused to accomplish the objective. Medium-low risk tolerant. Need an established vision. Good at organizing. Are process-oriented. Control various aspects of projects. Think short-term.)*
- ❏ **Reckoner** *(Focused on rules and accountability. Low risk tolerance. Organized and orderly. Have a set of standards they want to be followed. Gets things done in the most efficient way possible. Has excellent attention to detail.)*
- ❏ **Peddler** *(Focused on promotion of ideas. Medium-high risk tolerant. Achievement orientation. Friendly and likable. Assertive. High emotional intelligence.)*
- ❏ **Producer** *(Focused on doing the work. Medium-low risk-tolerant. Creativity is limited to the job at hand. Concrete thinkers. Low tolerance for ambiguity. Do not aspire to leadership positions. Separate work and personal life.)*

7. What are your strengths?

_____
_____
_____
_____
_____
_____
_____

- ❏ **Grower** *(Focused on novel ideas. High tolerance for risk and ambiguity. Energized by new prospects. Creative and seeing opportunities where others don't.)*
- ❏ **Chief** *(People focused on accomplishing the objective. Medium-high risk-tolerant. Create a vision for others. Good at coaching and mentoring. Change agents. Willing to try new things. Influence the process. Understand a team is more effective than individuals.)*
- ❏ **Implementor** *(Tasked focused to accomplish the objective. Medium-low risk tolerant. Need an established vision. Good at organizing. Are process-oriented. Control various aspects of projects. Think short-term.)*
- ❏ **Reckoner** *(Focused on rules and accountability. Low risk tolerance. Organized and orderly. Have a set of standards they want to be followed. Gets things done in the most efficient way possible. Has excellent attention to detail.)*
- ❏ **Peddler** *(Focused on promotion of ideas. Medium-high risk tolerant. Achievement orientation. Friendly and likable. Assertive. High emotional intelligence.)*
- ❏ **Producer** *(Focused on doing the work. Medium-low risk-tolerant. Creativity is limited to the job at hand. Concrete thinkers. Low tolerance for ambiguity. Do not aspire to leadership positions. Separate work and personal life.)*

8. Give an example of how you solved a problem in the past.

_____
_____
_____
_____
_____
_____
_____

- ❏ **Grower** *(Focused on novel ideas. High tolerance for risk and ambiguity. Energized by new prospects. Creative and seeing opportunities where others don't.)*
- ❏ **Chief** *(People focused on accomplishing the objective. Medium-high risk-tolerant. Create a vision for others. Good at coaching and mentoring. Change agents. Willing to try new things. Influence the process. Understand a team is more effective than individuals.)*
- ❏ **Implementor** *(Tasked focused to accomplish the objective. Medium-low risk tolerant. Need an established vision. Good at organizing. Are process-oriented. Control various aspects of projects. Think short-term.)*
- ❏ **Reckoner** *(Focused on rules and accountability. Low risk tolerance. Organized and orderly. Have a set of standards they want to be followed. Gets things done in the most efficient way possible. Has excellent attention to detail.)*
- ❏ **Peddler** *(Focused on promotion of ideas. Medium-high risk tolerant. Achievement orientation. Friendly and likable. Assertive. High emotional intelligence.)*
- ❏ **Producer** *(Focused on doing the work. Medium-low risk-tolerant. Creativity is limited to the job at hand. Concrete thinkers. Low tolerance for ambiguity. Do not aspire to leadership positions. Separate work and personal life.)*

9. What do you consider your best accomplishment in your last job?

_____
_____
_____
_____
_____
_____

- ❏ **Grower** *(Focused on novel ideas. High tolerance for risk and ambiguity. Energized by new prospects. Creative and seeing opportunities where others don't.)*
- ❏ **Chief** *(People focused on accomplishing the objective. Medium-high risk-tolerant. Create a vision for others. Good at coaching and mentoring. Change agents. Willing to try new things. Influence the process. Understand a team is more effective than individuals.)*
- ❏ **Implementor** *(Tasked focused to accomplish the objective. Medium-low risk tolerant. Need an established vision. Good at organizing. Are process-oriented. Control various aspects of projects. Think short-term.)*
- ❏ **Reckoner** *(Focused on rules and accountability. Low risk tolerance. Organized and orderly. Have a set of standards they want to be followed. Gets things done in the most efficient way possible. Has excellent attention to detail.)*
- ❏ **Peddler** *(Focused on promotion of ideas. Medium-high risk tolerant. Achievement orientation. Friendly and likable. Assertive. High emotional intelligence.)*
- ❏ **Producer** *(Focused on doing the work. Medium-low risk-tolerant. Creativity is limited to the job at hand. Concrete thinkers. Low tolerance for ambiguity. Do not aspire to leadership positions. Separate work and personal life.)*

10. Think about something you consider a work failure in your life and tell me why you think it happened.

_____
_____
_____
_____
_____
_____
_____

- ❏ **Grower** *(Focused on novel ideas. High tolerance for risk and ambiguity. Energized by new prospects. Creative and seeing opportunities where others don't.)*
- ❏ **Chief** *(People focused on accomplishing the objective. Medium-high risk-tolerant. Create a vision for others. Good at coaching and mentoring. Change agents. Willing to try new things. Influence the process. Understand a team is more effective than individuals.)*
- ❏ **Implementor** *(Tasked focused to accomplish the objective. Medium-low risk tolerant. Need an established vision. Good at organizing. Are process-oriented. Control various aspects of projects. Think short-term.)*
- ❏ **Reckoner** *(Focused on rules and accountability. Low risk tolerance. Organized and orderly. Have a set of standards they want to be followed. Gets things done in the most efficient way possible. Has excellent attention to detail.)*
- ❏ **Peddler** *(Focused on promotion of ideas. Medium-high risk tolerant. Achievement orientation. Friendly and likable. Assertive. High emotional intelligence.)*
- ❏ **Producer** *(Focused on doing the work. Medium-low risk-tolerant. Creativity is limited to the job at hand. Concrete thinkers. Low tolerance for ambiguity. Do not aspire to leadership positions. Separate work and personal life.)*

11. Give an example of when you were able to contribute to a team project.

_____
_____
_____
_____
_____
_____
_____

- ❏ **Grower** *(Focused on novel ideas. High tolerance for risk and ambiguity. Energized by new prospects. Creative and seeing opportunities where others don't.)*
- ❏ **Chief** *(People focused on accomplishing the objective. Medium-high risk-tolerant. Create a vision for others. Good at coaching and mentoring. Change agents. Willing to try new things. Influence the process. Understand a team is more effective than individuals.)*
- ❏ **Implementor** *(Tasked focused to accomplish the objective. Medium-low risk tolerant. Need an established vision. Good at organizing. Are process-oriented. Control various aspects of projects. Think short-term.)*
- ❏ **Reckoner** *(Focused on rules and accountability. Low risk tolerance. Organized and orderly. Have a set of standards they want to be followed. Gets things done in the most efficient way possible. Has excellent attention to detail.)*
- ❏ **Peddler** *(Focused on promotion of ideas. Medium-high risk tolerant. Achievement orientation. Friendly and likable. Assertive. High emotional intelligence.)*
- ❏ **Producer** *(Focused on doing the work. Medium-low risk-tolerant. Creativity is limited to the job at hand. Concrete thinkers. Low tolerance for ambiguity. Do not aspire to leadership positions. Separate work and personal life.)*

12. What unique skills do you bring to a team? Give an example.

_____
_____
_____
_____
_____
_____
_____

- ❏ **Grower** *(Focused on novel ideas. High tolerance for risk and ambiguity. Energized by new prospects. Creative and seeing opportunities where others don't.)*
- ❏ **Chief** *(People focused on accomplishing the objective. Medium-high risk-tolerant. Create a vision for others. Good at coaching and mentoring. Change agents. Willing to try new things. Influence the process. Understand a team is more effective than individuals.)*
- ❏ **Implementor** *(Tasked focused to accomplish the objective. Medium-low risk tolerant. Need an established vision. Good at organizing. Are process-oriented. Control various aspects of projects. Think short-term.)*
- ❏ **Reckoner** *(Focused on rules and accountability. Low risk tolerance. Organized and orderly. Have a set of standards they want to be followed. Gets things done in the most efficient way possible. Has excellent attention to detail.)*
- ❏ **Peddler** *(Focused on promotion of ideas. Medium-high risk tolerant. Achievement orientation. Friendly and likable. Assertive. High emotional intelligence.)*
- ❏ **Producer** *(Focused on doing the work. Medium-low risk-tolerant. Creativity is limited to the job at hand. Concrete thinkers. Low tolerance for ambiguity. Do not aspire to leadership positions. Separate work and personal life.)*

13. What can you do day after day without tiring?

_____
_____
_____
_____
_____
_____

- ❏ **Grower** *(Focused on novel ideas. High tolerance for risk and ambiguity. Energized by new prospects. Creative and seeing opportunities where others don't.)*
- ❏ **Chief** *(People focused on accomplishing the objective. Medium-high risk-tolerant. Create a vision for others. Good at coaching and mentoring. Change agents. Willing to try new things. Influence the process. Understand a team is more effective than individuals.)*
- ❏ **Implementor** *(Tasked focused to accomplish the objective. Medium-low risk tolerant. Need an established vision. Good at organizing. Are process-oriented. Control various aspects of projects. Think short-term.)*
- ❏ **Reckoner** *(Focused on rules and accountability. Low risk tolerance. Organized and orderly. Have a set of standards they want to be followed. Gets things done in the most efficient way possible. Has excellent attention to detail.)*
- ❏ **Peddler** *(Focused on promotion of ideas. Medium-high risk tolerant. Achievement orientation. Friendly and likable. Assertive. High emotional intelligence.)*
- ❏ **Producer** *(Focused on doing the work. Medium-low risk-tolerant. Creativity is limited to the job at hand. Concrete thinkers. Low tolerance for ambiguity. Do not aspire to leadership positions. Separate work and personal life.)*

14. Tell me about a time you felt you were in the wrong job or that someone else could do your job better than you.

_____
_____
_____
_____
_____
_____

- ❏ **Grower** *(Focused on novel ideas. High tolerance for risk and ambiguity. Energized by new prospects. Creative and seeing opportunities where others don't.)*
- ❏ **Chief** *(People focused on accomplishing the objective. Medium-high risk-tolerant. Create a vision for others. Good at coaching and mentoring. Change agents. Willing to try new things. Influence the process. Understand a team is more effective than individuals.)*
- ❏ **Implementor** *(Tasked focused to accomplish the objective. Medium-low risk tolerant. Need an established vision. Good at organizing. Are process-oriented. Control various aspects of projects. Think short-term.)*
- ❏ **Reckoner** *(Focused on rules and accountability. Low risk tolerance. Organized and orderly. Have a set of standards they want to be followed. Gets things done in the most efficient way possible. Has excellent attention to detail.)*
- ❏ **Peddler** *(Focused on promotion of ideas. Medium-high risk tolerant. Achievement orientation. Friendly and likable. Assertive. High emotional intelligence.)*
- ❏ **Producer** *(Focused on doing the work. Medium-low risk-tolerant. Creativity is limited to the job at hand. Concrete thinkers. Low tolerance for ambiguity. Do not aspire to leadership positions. Separate work and personal life.)*

Your overall impressions of this applicant.

_____
_____
_____
_____
_____

Based on your impression and the applicant's answers, mark the most apparent innate ability:

- ❏ **Grower** *(Focused on novel ideas. High tolerance for risk and ambiguity. Energized by new prospects. Creative and seeing opportunities where others don't.)*
- ❏ **Chief** *(People focused on accomplishing the objective. Medium-high risk-tolerant. Create a vision for others. Good at coaching and mentoring. Change agents. Willing to try new things. Influence the process. Understand a team is more effective than individuals.)*
- ❏ **Implementor** *(Tasked focused to accomplish the objective. Medium-low risk tolerant. Need an established vision. Good at organizing. Are process-oriented. Control various aspects of projects. Think short-term.)*
- ❏ **Reckoner** *(Focused on rules and accountability. Low risk tolerance. Organized and orderly. Have a set of standards they want to be followed. Gets things done in the most efficient way possible. Has excellent attention to detail.)*
- ❏ **Peddler** *(Focused on promotion of ideas. Medium-high risk tolerant. Achievement orientation. Friendly and likable. Assertive. High emotional intelligence.)*
- ❏ **Producer** *(Focused on doing the work. Medium-low risk-tolerant. Creativity is limited to the job at hand. Concrete thinkers. Low tolerance for ambiguity. Do not aspire to leadership positions. Separate work and personal life.)*

You can add or delete whatever questions you want. The example is only meant to illustrate how you can incorporate the template into your existing interview questions. If multiple interviewers are involved, compare answers. Is there a consensus? Look at the applicant's self-rating that you had them complete. Where did they rate themselves? Note, the list they rank-ordered themselves is in order of grower, chief, implementor, reckoner, peddler, and producer.

You are golden if the person meets the job requirements for the position and whatever else you are looking for and has the innate ability you want. That person is the best candidate. Hire them.

APPENDIX B

The Promoting Template

If you are promoting from within, you might already know the person's innate ability. If not, have them complete the following:

Self-Rating

Order from 1 to 6, most like you to least like you, with 1 being most like you and 6 being least like you. Use each number, but only once. *(There is no right order. We just want to get to know you a little better.)*

On the job, your focus is best:

____on coming up with novel solutions.

____on the people who need to be mobilized to accomplish a goal.

____on lining out the tasks that are needed to be completed.

____on making sure the company is accountable.

____on broadcasting the successful outcomes to others.

____on doing the work that's needed.

You can conduct an interview if your company engages in a formal procedure. You can use something like the sample question provided in appendix A. You can also gather a group that knows the person and have each reflect on the person. Based on their knowledge, mark the template.

- **Grower** *(Focused on novel ideas. High tolerance for risk and ambiguity. Energized by new prospects. Creative and seeing opportunities where others don't.)*
- **Chief** *(People focused on accomplishing the objective. Medium-high risk-tolerant. Create a vision for others. Good at coaching and mentoring. Change agents. Willing to try new things. Influence the process. Understand a team is more effective than individuals.)*
- **Implementor** *(Tasked focused to accomplish the objective. Medium-low risk tolerant. Need an established vision. Good at organizing. Are process-oriented. Control various aspects of projects. Think short-term.)*
- **Reckoner** *(Focused on rules and accountability. Low risk tolerance. Organized and orderly. Have a set of standards they want to be followed. Gets things done in the most efficient way possible. Has excellent attention to detail.)*
- **Peddler** *(Focused on promotion of ideas. Medium-high risk tolerant. Achievement orientation. Friendly and likable. Assertive. High emotional intelligence.)*
- **Producer** *(Focused on doing the work. Medium-low risk-tolerant. Creativity is limited to the job at hand. Concrete thinkers. Low tolerance for ambiguity. Do not aspire to leadership positions. Separate work and personal life.)*

www.ingramcontent.com/pod-product-compliance
Lightning Source LLC
LaVergne TN
LVHW041608070526
838199LV00052B/3046